RAZING AFRICVILLE:
A GEOGRAPHY OF RACISM

In the 1960s, the city of Halifax demolished the black community of Africville, ostensibly as part of a program of urban renewal and 'slum clearance.' The city defended its actions by citing the deplorable living conditions in Africville, ignoring its own role in the creation of these conditions through years of neglect and denial of essential services. In the 1980s, the city created a park on the empty site, which has since become a place of protest and commemoration for black citizens. As yet the city has not issued a formal apology to Africville residents and has paid no further compensation.

Razing Africville examines the history of the eviction of a community from its own space. Examining accounts from a variety of sources – urban planning texts, city council documents, news media, and academic reports – Jennifer J. Nelson illustrates how Africville went from a slum to an urban problem to be addressed and, more recently, to a public space in which past abuses are rendered invisible. Reading historical texts as a critical map of decision-making, she argues that the ongoing measures taken to regulate black bodies and spaces contribute to a 'geography of racism.' She analyses ways in which space is tied to racial identity and domination and how the control of space is a necessary component of delineating and regulating populations.

A much-needed re-examination of an important chapter in Canadian history, *Razing Africville* applies spatial theory analysis to the destruction of a community, and offers critical observations on racism and its function in our society.

JENNIFER J. NELSON is an independent research consultant based in Toronto.

JENNIFER J. NELSON

Razing Africville

A Geography of Racism

UNIVERSITY OF TORONTO PRESS
Toronto Buffalo London

Reprinted in paperback 2009, 2011

ISBN 978-0-8020-9252-6 (cloth)
ISBN 978-1-4426-1028-6 (paper)

Printed on acid-free paper.

Library and Archives Canada Cataloguing in Publication

Nelson, Jennifer J. (Jennifer Jill), 1972–
Razing Africville : a geography of racism / Jennifer J. Nelson.

Includes bibliographical references and index.
ISBN 978-0-8020-9252-6 (bound).–ISBN 978-1-4426-1028-6 (pbk.)

1. Africville (Halifax, N.S.)–History. 2. Racism–Government policy–Nova
Scotia–Halifax–History. 3. Blacks–Relocation–Nova Scotia–Halifax–Histo-
ry. 4. Whites–Race identity–Nova Scotia–Halifax. 5. Blacks–Race identity–
Nova Scotia–Halifax. 6. Halifax (N.S.)–History. I. Title.

FC2346.9.N4N45 2007   971.6'22504   C2007-903920-0

University of Toronto Press acknowledges the financial assistance to its
publishing program of the Canada Council for the Arts and the Ontario
Arts Council.

University of Toronto Press acknowledges the financial support for its publishing activities of the Government of Canada through the Book Publishing Industry Development Program (BPIDP).

Cover photograph: Slums of Africville, 1958, Halifax, N.S. © Canada
Mortgage and Housing Corporation. Reproduced with the permission of
the Minister of Public Works and Government Services Canada (2007).
Library and Archives Canada/Central Mortgage and Housing Corporation
(Canada) collection/PA- 170736

If you don't know my name, then you don't know your own.

James Baldwin

Contents

Acknowledgments

The project on which this book is based has now spanned almost a decade. In this time, I have relied on countless individuals and various modes of support, from the intellectual to the emotional to the very practical – none of which can be stressed enough.

My family, friends, and colleagues have all contributed to seeing me through this work and to making it what it is. I especially thank Sherene Razack, who thought she was finished with me after my dissertation, for her ongoing interest and encouragement to publish. I have continued to draw upon her passion and her brilliantly incisive critical gaze while making revisions. The early invaluable contributions from my dissertation committee have also seen their way well into the final work. The thoughtful engagement shown by Ruth Roach Pearson, Kari Dehli, and Nicholas Blomley offered insight and wisdom well beyond the call.

This research was supported by a four-year fellowship from the Social Sciences and Humanities Research Council of Canada and I remain very grateful for their support.

While it is standard to thank one's peer referees, I truly cannot say enough about mine. I owe much to the three anonymous reviewers who took the time to engage in such depth with this work. All were respectful and supportive while offering the most constructive criticism. I felt I was in conversation with them as I completed the manuscript.

My editor at University of Toronto Press, Virgil Duff, has been nothing but dedicated and helpful throughout the publication process, patiently and promptly responding to my two thousand 'new author' questions regarding 'what happens next?' (He was also responsible, of course, for finding those excellent peer reviewers.) Mary Newberry worked as both an early consultant and, later, my copy editor. Her footprint is throughout these pages; her attention to detail and her ability to decipher and clarify many threads of argument at once are rare gifts.

I thank Manon Labrecque, another expert on details, for her keen interest, support and bibliographic assistance. I have also relied immeasurably on the friendship and insight of Donna Jeffery, who has always kindly reminded me that this book was worth pursuing and that it would actually, one day, be finished.

My early work on this project benefited greatly from the support and encouragement of Doreen Fumia, Zoe Newman, Donna Jeffery, Sheila Gill and Laura Cleghorn, all of who were instrumental in fostering my ideas, and in sustaining me while I attempted to turn them into something intelligible. On this count, many connections with colleagues at OISE/UT have enriched my learning and continue to challenge me.

I thank Nancy Nelson, Tony Colaiacovo, and Kevin Davison for being dedicated 'Halifax correspondents' during my research, sending much-needed articles and information across the miles. And when I was able to do it firsthand, the staff at the Public Archives of Nova Scotia, the Halifax Regional Library, and the Black Cultural Centre were incredibly helpful, showing interest and patience as I monopolized great volumes of their collections.

Finally, but certainly not least, I thank my husband, Andrew, for what is now nearly a decade of love and support in my work and the rest of life.

I dedicate this book to my parents, Joyce (Tingley) Nelson (1932–85) and Harry Nelson (1930–85), and to my grandmother Winnie (Carpenter) Tingley (1909–2003).

A hundred times every day I remind myself that my inner and outer life are based on the labors of others.

Albert Einstein

RAZING AFRICVILLE:
A GEOGRAPHY OF RACISM

1 Authoring Africville: A Selected History

Replying 'Africville' to a question about my work tends to elicit an impassioned response. It is a well-known story – at least in eastern Canada – and many individuals have their version at hand: It was a shame, a tragedy. The city had no choice. It was a slum. It was the era of integration. What ever happened to those people? We didn't want to leave. It's shocking. It isn't surprising. It was only because we were black. They're terribly bitter. They can't forget the past. It will never happen again … Other responses betray the ease with which ugly moments in history get erased from public consciousness: Really? That's hard to believe! When? Afric-what?

To quickly fill in history's blank spaces, I find myself supplying the abbreviated form: Africville was a black community in Halifax, Nova Scotia, on the east coast of Canada, that was bulldozed by the city during the 1960s. I move on to attempt to answer what follows: How? Why? And what would motivate me to write about that? These questions, simple and logical, are the most important ones.

As with any account, opinions vary with individual and group histories, wavering as we draw nearer or farther away. For me, it is a story both immediate and remote. For an academic writer attempting to think critically about race, it is both a crucial moment in the nation's history of racism and an ongoing struggle for justice. As a white woman from a working-class, rural town in Nova Scotia, I see Africville as a shadow of the past, mirroring the black community near my own home. Africville is far removed from my experience, yet it is inseparable from the history of white settlement, which shaped its evolution and foreshadowed its destruction.

White perspectives on the many variations of the story are often characterized by a mixture of pity, regret, shame, defensiveness, and anger. A common belief is that Africville's destruction was an unfortunate incident that was born of a necessary and humanitarian effort. This perspective is accompanied by a sense that the past must be forgotten, that 'we,' and therefore 'they,' must move on. But what is at stake in forgetting the past? Simply put, why should anyone be concerned with Africville today? Some of the answers seem apparent: it is a monumental example of racism at work in Canadian history; it had a devastating effect on the black community; it is a relatively recent event; it is not 'over' – in the sense that nothing has really been done about it; it is not unique – racialized communities are neglected, denied, destroyed all the time. I think it could, and absolutely would, happen again. It is both shocking and ordinary at the same time. Perhaps the key challenge in writing about it is to hold both aspects in balance: to demonstrate the matter-of-fact banality of racism that belies shock, while conveying the very ugliness and violence of that banality.

Africville's removal was a planned and widely sanctioned destruction, a clearance, a razing, of black space, of black people. It didn't happen suddenly; it wasn't surprising. It also wasn't unique. Other stories of forced removals and relocations abound, and they speak to similar, yet time- and place-specific, assertions and configurations of white domination in post-colonial North America. For example, a large body of literature examines the internment of Japanese Canadians and Japanese Americans during the 1940s.[1] Various scholars have detailed the destruction of Aboriginal communities, not just during early colonization but throughout the twentieth century, often under the rubric of industrial development programs like the Kinzua Dam project on the Mississippi River in the 1960s.[2] Various Inuit-relocation programs in the Canadian Arctic have been analysed, such as the forced relocation of the Sayisi Dene from their traditional territories in present-day northern Manitoba.[3]

Many studies have examined the issues of race, urban renewal, housing, and planning in twentieth-century North America.[4] This literature is replete with stories of forced relocation under the banner of slum clearance. These events mostly occurred at around the same time as the razing of Africville and bear a close resemblance to its destruction. The city of Chicago removed black communities around the University of Chicago during the 1950s,[5] as did the city of Charlottesville, Virginia, in its destruction of Vinegar Hill during the 1960s.[6] A new university displaced African American residents in near-Westside, Indianapolis, in the 1960s,[7] and the city of Atlanta destroyed the homes of over 55,000 black residents during its downtown regeneration program of the same era.[8] These are but a few examples of an urban renewal movement that swept North America during the mid-twentieth century.[9]

In light of such an extended geography of destruction, I have come to see Africville not as an isolated event in history. Rather, it *is* history. The nation does not exist above or around Africville, nor does the nation contain Africville; rather, the nation came to be through Africville's regulation, as through other kinds of violence. When we begin to grasp the significance of racialized spaces and their regulation to the fabric of Canadian society, there is no disconnection between present daily social life and the past on which it stands. The common sense–making practices that lie behind marginality, dominance, and hierarchy figure in all of our individual and collective histories, albeit in markedly different and unequal ways.

I have written this book from a particular point of view – that the razing of Africville is a story of white domination, a story of the making of a slum, and of the operation of technologies of oppression and regulation over time. This study frames Africville as both an image in the white imagination and a concrete place against which progress and respectability are measured, and around which borders, real and symbolic, are placed. I see Africville's destruction as a deliberate moment within a larger colonial project of spatial management. I posit that certain (black) bodies are consistently produced as marginal within various facets of dominant white culture, such as media, education, academic work, and governmental discourse. I trace the regulation of black bodies and spaces with a view to how whites come to know themselves in relation to this regulation, and through their subsequent portrayal of their own actions. This is one of perhaps a very few angles from which I, as a white person, can approach an intimate, violent black experience. To ignore it is to remain complicit in forgetting, while to retell it is to suggest it has not already been told by those who know first-hand, or to intrude on an experience not mine to articulate.

I look closely at the actions and words of whites in positions of authority in and around the Africville decision – that is, the academic studies, urban planning and social work reports, city council discussions, journalism, and mainstream news that shaped how blacks were viewed and portrayed by whites in Nova Scotia shortly before, during, and after the destruction of Africville. This introductory chapter provides a brief history of events leading up to Africville's establishment and removal. It also situates my reading of Africville's destruction at the juncture of knowledge production, spatial regulation, and racist ideology in a particular time and place. This introduction begins the work of illustrating how I have taken on the fundamental questions: How? Why? And why write about it?

Rooted in Nova Scotia

Eight years ago, early in the research for this work, I returned to Halifax to visit Africville's former site. I walked along gravel paths through the rolling slopes of a brown-green park at the edge of the ocean on a grey day in March. Bitter maritime winds stung my face. The cries of gulls and the background din of traffic was muted in the damp harbour air. Two or three other souls, hunched in layers of clothes against the wind, wandered across the grass and approached the harbourside for a look at the water. On that day, I struggled to realize that the site before me constituted the ground where Africville once stood: its contours have been altered, and there is little to suggest its history.

Facing west, I feel part of an urban centre; east, I am a witness to the bustle of a sprawling naval base. But in the immediate vicinity, I am a small figure in a space that seems empty. To the south is the port where my first Danish ancestor escaped from a British press gang to form a family network in the northwest region of the province. For over two hundred years, my family, formed from this relocated Dane and various Northern Irish, German, and white Loyalist settlers, farmed these lands, built streets and fountains to mark the footprint of their commissioners, and placed monuments in recognition of public celebration and private grief. I am rooted in this rugged, austere corner of the world where I find the archeology of my life at almost every turn – when I see Londonderry on the map, when I come across the sundial my father built in Halifax's Public Gardens, and when I visit any cemetery and see the markers of my family commemorating the past.

I did not learn about Africville in school, in my small town an hour from Halifax. I learned about my own history, sitting next to kids from Panuke Road, the 'black area' outside of town. It didn't feel like my history at the time; it was mostly about kings and queens and wars, not farmers and stonecutters. Then it was about faceless colonists who bravely crossed the ocean and settled this wild territory, empty save for a few Indians. Such tales never seemed connected to me, to the present, to Africville, to Panuke Road. Yet, in its manicured form, Africville is now offered to me, too; its space has been rendered public, 'neutral.' I am invited to enjoy the scene, the ocean wind, the sanitized tribute to history on the nearby monument – suggesting Africville, but concealing its story. This is, in a city official's words, 'a place for young and old, a place to dream their dreams.' But to whose dreams does he refer? Surely not those of the black families who settled here for over a century before their community was destroyed. Surely not the dreams of black children who once spent their summers at the water's edge, diving into the basin. This is a space from which those children were expelled, on which their story must fight to speak itself, and to which they are now invited back as guests, permitted to dream until the next eviction forbids that too. At the edge of the harbour, Africville's death is concealed, rewritten.

I grew up visiting cemeteries with my father, as he and his brothers designed and built monuments. I have never found them strange or morbid. But this one is different. I have no obvious connection to Africville's grave site, to the stone marking this death. Why, then, the nagging sense that Africville has everything to do with my history too? Why the sense that there is more to learn from this site than of its life and death, more than its Otherness in time and space? How might history be read so that the complex, uneven connections between white lives and black lives are visible?

The establishment of Nova Scotia as a British domain and a world naval base did not come about easily. White settlement here, as in North America generally, followed a long and complex path characterized by violence, racial segregation, and ethnic and class struggle. While a thorough illustration of this history is beyond the scope of this book, some particularities are worth noting in brief in order to draw the contours of racism under which Africville developed.

Of all regions in Canada, Nova Scotia saw the largest migration of blacks following both the American Revolutionary War and the War of 1812. Prior to the shifting immigration patterns of the last few decades, it was known as the hub of Canada's black citizenry. The descendants of these early populations make up the majority of the province's black residents today.

For geographic reasons, namely the rocky soil and harsh climate, plantation slavery never developed on a large scale in Nova Scotia.

Still, whites practised slavery throughout the province from as early as the sixteenth century, when Portuguese and French explorers began enslaving Aboriginal peoples. Records show that a few black slaves existed in the province at this time as well, but the importation of blacks into Canada for the purpose of slave labour was officially sanctioned in 1689 by King Louis XIV of France.[10] However, the labour requirements of the fur trade were inconsistent with slavery, and the lack of plantation industry, accompanied by indifference on the part of the Roman Catholic Church, meant that little importation followed. By contrast, when the British established rule in 1760 they incorporated slavery into the treaty by which the government changed hands, and the English Protestant churches were more supportive of the institution. Slavery was reinforced by an imperial law in 1790 under which the government encouraged incoming citizens to bring their slaves along with 'other property.'

The processes facilitating an increase in slavery had begun even earlier in Nova Scotia, where the British, who retained the lands of Acadie from the French in 1713, offered settlement opportunities to New England immigrants who brought slaves with them. By mid-century the continuing struggle over territory between France and Britain had escalated; the British expelled over eight thousand French Acadians who refused to swear loyalty to the British crown. Their confiscated lands, formerly inhabited by the Mi'kmaq, opened the way for more English settlers and the number of slaves in the province reached about five hundred.

Records indicate that black slaves worked on the construction of Fort Louisbourg in Cape Breton, and in Halifax from the time of its founding in 1749. Numerous papers from eighteenth-century Halifax advertise the sale of slaves, and the years of Loyalist migration in 1783 and 1784 saw not only an increase in their numbers by twelve hundred,[11] but in the replacement of Aboriginal peoples with blacks in these roles. This replacement coincided with the ongoing displacement of the Mi'kmaq, whose land the government seized throughout the eighteenth century. When the Mi'kmaq refused to relinquish entitlement to their territories, and resisted the terms of English-language treaties that had been unclear to them upon signing, the British retaliated with a campaign of bounty-hunting and imprisonment of Mi'kmaq peoples. The British placed most Mi'kmaq on reserve lands by the early 1800s, by which time the population had been decimated through starvation and from dependence on the French for European goods, including alcohol, and through the decline of traditional hunting and trading. These factors were, of course, augmented by genocide and the transfer and spread of disease from Europe.[12]

Due to its location as a naval base only six hundred miles from New York, its existing core of former New England residents, and its sparse population, Nova Scotia was deemed an ideal site for the resettlement of Loyalist immigrants. Altogether, about 3500 free blacks migrated to the region, many of whom had promised their loyalty to the British army in return for freedom. While white Loyalists holding upper class or military status received sizeable plots of land suitable for farming, poor whites were often forced to wait several years for their land. The colonial government forced free blacks to settle outside the major towns in segregated areas. When they were given land at all, it was of the poorest quality, rocky and infertile. Their plots were significantly smaller than those of whites, and the government, in most cases, failed to fulfil a promise of free food and supplies for the first three years.[13] Blacks were often required to prove their intent to settle for several years before being granted legal title. This precluded selling their properties and relocating to more productive areas. It also allowed the government great freedom in reappropriating their lands and thus controlling the province's patterns of industrial and residential development along racial lines.

After 1800, it became increasingly difficult to hold slaves in Nova Scotia. The decline, which lead to slavery's official illegality in 1834, was due in part to public opposition, but also to an increase in the available labour pool of free Loyalist blacks and whites whose services could be bought for even less than the price of keeping slaves. Some slave proprietors strongly opposed the struggle for abolition into the early 1800s, drawing petitions to request the maintenance of the institution, to secure their 'personal property.' Slave-owners demanded financial compensation for any slaves removed from them, and the government began to install regulations for the gradual release of slaves, often according to age and length of term served. There are no records of compensation having been granted following their release.[14]

While slavery as a system faded in this period, the conditions of life for black workers seem to have changed only marginally with their alternative forms of livelihood. The thirty thousand Loyalist migrants had more than tripled the population of Nova Scotia, placing enormous demands on government resources. Many white settlers lived under deplorable conditions, yet promises of land and assistance to black Loyalists were, predictably, even more elusive. Jobs were scarce, and competition between black and poor white residents was fierce. The fact that the labour of blacks was undervalued economically by white employers fuelled the bitterness of lower-class whites who felt that blacks' lower remuneration undermined their opportunities. This resentment contributed to race riots in the Shelburne area in 1784, during which whites pursued blacks to their settlement at Birchtown and proceeded to destroy many of their homes.[15] Historical accounts exist of several riots,[16] and many individual cases of violence against black servants have also been documented.[17]

The provincial House of Assembly, strongly opposed to the imperial government's acceptance of refugee blacks, cited 'Africans' as a liability, perilous to the immigration of 'decent white labourers and servants.'[18] The legacy of slavery contributed to a notion of black refugees as unfit for employment.[19] Following the settlement of the free Loyalist blacks, a number would be forced to sell themselves and their children back into slavery or to become, in the common terminology of the time, 'indentured servants.' Those who had settled near major towns were sometimes able to find waged labour at about one quarter of the rate paid to whites performing the same work. Others found work as tenant farmers on white-owned lands, where they were often moved and resettled as needed. Overall, black workers were instrumental in clearing the bulk of Nova Scotian lands and constructing the majority of roads and buildings.[20]

Due to the paucity of arable land and the provincial government's apparent indifference, a number of black residents seized an opportunity for emigration offered by the Sierra Leone company in 1791. Almost twelve hundred sailed to Sierra Leone the following year, leaving the province's population of free blacks lower than that of its indentured servants. Within four years, a group of 550 Maroons, refugees deported by the government of Jamaica for their rebellion against slavery, had settled on the black Loyalists' vacated lands in the Preston area, outside Halifax. The Maroons were supported financially by the Jamaican government and were known for their physical strength and military acumen; they were a welcome source of labour in rebuilding the Halifax Citadel. However, they strongly resisted Christian teachings, servitude in white homes, and threats to their group identity. Like the former occupants of their lands, the Maroons found the harsh climate and poor soil a major barrier to productivity, and were unable to achieve financial self-sufficiency. When their requests to be relocated to another part of the British Empire were ignored, the Maroons adopted a strategy of resistance and non-cooperation, refusing to work on public projects. The Jamaican government withdrew support after the first year, and the province forcibly shipped the Maroons to Sierra Leone in 1800.

Even in brief, it is clear that Nova Scotia's historical patterns of settlement have been characterized by the regulation, confinement, and upheaval of its Aboriginal and minority populations. All disputes over territory share a foundation in the original dispossession of Native peoples. The Acadians lived on Mi'kmaq lands, and thus these areas were appropriated not once but twice; similarly, the lands allotted to black migrants were neither within the rightful jurisdiction of the British to distribute, nor in possession of the black settlers. However, it is crucial to keep in mind the histories by which these groups came to occupy the lands – the former landed unannounced and forcibly claimed the territory, the latter were, variably, exiled or escaped peoples struggling for survival. Many blacks came unwillingly, and those who selected Nova Scotia as their home did so within a severely limited range of choices. Blacks share with the Mi'kmaq, and with the Acadians, histories of physical and psychological abuse through the destruction of their communities and ways of life. Governing Europeans considered them ultimately expendable, their territories unoccupied and available for exploitation. The black settlers became accustomed, early, to a persistent underlying instability that comes of tenuous land occupancy, meagre resources, and the constant underlying threat of violence. Nova Scotia's character as a reluctant host, a repository for 'deviants,' or a temporary refuge for unwelcome visitors before their expulsion to other lands was firmly in place long before Africville was uprooted and bulldozed.

In 1815, former lands of the black Loyalists and Maroons were made available to black refugees from the War of 1812. The government had hoped the refugees would supply Halifax with fresh produce, but soil conditions were hardly conducive to agriculture. The opportunities of these free blacks were further impeded when they were awarded only 'licences of occupation' rather than title to their infertile land. While they had been promised legal title after inhabiting the space for three years, it was twenty-seven years before the government fulfilled this agreement; only then could these settlers sell their plots and consider relocating.

Africville was founded by these refugees and their descendants. In the 1840s, they purchased properties on the shore of the Bedford Basin from white merchants, several of whom had been slave-traders. Here, the new residents fished, began keeping livestock, and explored opportunities for waged labour in the nearby city. Within a few years they had built a Baptist church. After petitioning for educational resources from the city for over twenty years, they were able to establish their own school. Properties in the community were handed down within families, and family members often constructed new homes near those of relatives. Men found work as stevedores in the nearby dockyards, or as stonemasons, truck drivers, and seamen, while women frequently performed domestic work in white households or government institutions. The establishment of a separate post office and several small stores contributed to the community's self-sufficiency.

As Halifax expanded, particularly in the latter half of the nineteenth century, various industries and businesses encroached on Africville land. The establishment of the Nova Scotia Railway Company in 1853 resulted in early demolition of several homes as rail lines were built through the community. Around the same time, the City of Halifax built its prison on the hill overlooking Africville, and placed its 'night soil' disposal pit on the eastern edge of Africville. The next decades saw the expansion of various industries in the area, including an oil plant storage facility, a bone mill, a cotton factory, two slaughterhouses, a tar factory, a coal handling facility, and a foundry. In the 1870s, the city built an infectious diseases hospital on the overlooking hill, and later added a trachoma hospital, the wastes from which poured onto Africville soil.

Following increased railway expansion during the early twentieth century, the city uprooted more Africville families and, after a 1947 rezoning, began to solidify plans to fully expropriate the lands for industrial use. In Africville's last decade, the city moved its dump directly onto the community's land. Two years later, an incinerator appeared only fifty yards beyond the south border of Africville.

Throughout Africville's existence, the city government frequently denied building permits to residents wishing to improve their homes. They also refused requests for water and sewage lines, garbage collection, police services, and fire protection. Newspapers from the time report dangerous conditions. Given the proximity of the dump, and deprived of proper heating, some residents burned discarded batteries for warmth, resulting in several cases of lead poisoning. Fires were frequent, resulting in injuries and deaths, as they could not be extinguished in an area with no water lines. The only action taken by the city against contamination in the water supply was to post a sign warning residents to boil the water before drinking and cooking. Some reports speculated that residents may have developed immunity to the copious bacteria in their wells.[21]

Ignoring the city's role in creating these conditions, government officials reasoned that the deplorable state of the community would soon necessitate its removal. They entered into a series of discussions with 'experts' who evaluated Africville similarly, and voted to demolish the community after only minimal, superficial consultation with residents. By the end of the 1960s, against the wishes of most residents, the city of Halifax had expropriated Africville.

Due to an informal system of handing down properties and housing within families and among in-laws over the years, many residents were unable to prove legal title to their land and had little recourse when faced with the choice to sell or be evicted. Even where fair prices were obtained for homes and land, compensation to homeowners who were now forced to move and pay rent was still inadequate. In many instances, financial remuneration was minimal. Africville had little formal community leadership, no political representation, and no access to the legal bargaining tools of the municipality. From the beginning, the so-called relocation[22] took a paternalistic approach, and was characterized by broken promises, bureaucratic disorganization, and lack of long-term planning. The dispersal of the residents into housing projects in the city's north end or in outlying areas, where many were forced to accept welfare payments and to pay rent for the first time in their lives, resulted in the obliteration of Africville.

During the 1980s and 1990s, the black community, sometimes alongside the city and white residents, held various commemorative events in Africville's honour. The 1980s saw the construction of the manicured park described earlier. Standing on a blanket of grass in 1999, I struggled to imagine the homes, roads, baseball field, church, outside in 1999, I lavatories, the dump. I have seen pictures, but to me they could be pictures of any place.

Terms of Engagement: Discursive Power

This book does not tell the story of a century and more of survival against racism. It is not a story of the pain of forced removal from one's home, or of the lived reality of Africville, which still ignites powerful resistance on the part of black Nova Scotians. Their stories are deeply personal, and have been told first-hand. My account, however, is quite different. It is, centrally, a struggle to understand how a racist act – the destruction of a community – occurs. This struggle demands that one grapple with a few different questions, and a few different bodies of theoretical work. What is it necessary to *know* about a community in order to destroy it? What does one need to know about oneself and one's own group, in relation to the community, in order to destroy it? How does this knowledge come about? How do whites realize in themselves the capacity to govern, to decide, to act? Frankly, what do they need to know about what was done, and how do they rationalize certain actions, in order to sleep at night? This is not a cynical question; it points to a serious need to understand how specific stories must be mobilized and vested with meaning so that actions make sense. The sense-making practices operative in Africville's destruction, I argue, are mobilized through discourses of *race* and *space*. Racism does not fully make sense until we understand regulated, spatialized social relations. Such relations are realized in and through violence, degradation, and poverty; they are concretized in the slum. And they rely on governing principles and practices that are not simply accepted at face value – that is, to study discourses about the motivations and decisions behind Africville's destruction requires a particular, critical lens. This is not to suggest that a unified set of conscious intentions existed and can be unearthed, but this work intends to disrupt the common assertion that officials and planners operated innocently with only the welfare of Africville residents at the heart of their project. In other words, I am not concerned with determining and labelling 'who was racist' in a conscious or deliberate sense. To understand more broadly, and, I believe, more usefully, how a historic moment occurs is to employ a set of conceptual tools that frames the question differently: How does power operate in such a way that certain actions and outcomes – and *not* other actions and outcomes – appear self-evident?

While my theoretical framework is more completely illustrated in chapter 2, I want to briefly introduce some key concepts and analytic tools that are employed throughout. I draw on the work of Michel Foucault, among others, to assert that knowledge cannot be considered outside its relationship to power. I follow Foucault in using the term 'discourse' as a group of statements that constitutes a set of understandings about a topic or phenomenon at a given historical moment. Discourses construct the topic itself and the meanings that surround it.

Discourses also define and govern what can be said, and imply or delineate what cannot be said, about a phenomenon.[23] For instance, what might be called the discourse of 'cultures of poverty' includes statements about the assumed resignation and hopelessness of marginalized, impoverished communities. It also relies on statements about the inherent characteristics of these communities, which often have racial- and gender-specific manifestations (calling to mind stereotypes about, for instance, 'welfare mothers' or 'violent young black men'). The phrase 'culture of poverty'[24] does not necessarily include or exclude any of these meanings; it does not, in Foucauldian terms, have an inherent meaning outside of discourse; therefore, we can say only that its particular, common meaning, at a given time and in a given context, takes this form and has this effect. The term appeared, for instance, in the mid-twentieth century, in the United States and Canada, and was used by political scientists, cultural and social theorists, and economists. It was picked up and circulated widely through the news media and by prominent politicians.

The dominance of 'culture of poverty' discourse can make it difficult to speak about alternative explanations for the proliferation of poverty – for instance, systemic racism, a history of slavery, ongoing socioeconomic discrimination, labour and class struggles, particular government policies, or the internalization of oppression over time. That some discourses come to be dominant, and are imbued with a sense of authority, is a function of *power*. Discourses congeal to form 'regimes of truth' – ways of viewing the world that become powerful and dominant, while their social and historical sites of production are obscured. They become 'common sense, taken-for-granted, axiomatic, traditional, normal.'[25] Statements become meaningful through discourse. By examining discourse, we look for the ways in which talk about a topic allows meanings to emerge, and how a statement garners the power to dominate, to render other meanings *untrue* or *unspeakable* – as in not able to be spoken – at a certain historical time.

Power, as I use the term, is not something that is possessed or held in particular bodies or places; it is, rather, accessed differently by different groups and individuals and *employed* in particular moments in a variety of ways. Power is not essentially negative or positive; rather, it is *productive*. Foucault described power as a 'netlike' mechanism enveloping social relations, circulating not simply through individuals but through social institutions. When I refer to governmental concern with the management and regulation of difference that is made possible by discursive practices, I am referencing Foucault's concept of govern-mentality; by this he defines the state not as a unified body which exerts power over its constituents, but as a labyrinth of the many agencies and institutions through which power relations and modes of governance are constituted.[26]

The news media and the education system are institutions through which a particular discourse might garner enough power to become dominant or commonly accepted. When I refer to racism as institution-alized, then, I am referencing sets of discourses about racial differences that have been imbued with power in Western societies, so that they have been accepted as truth. For example, a common discourse about 'violent young black men' has acquired enough authority to result in racial profiling and the over-policing of black communities. This doesn't mean that all people believe the discourse; there are critical, resistant discourses in circulation. It does mean that the discourse is powerfully operative in society, and that such forms of knowledge have consequences; they give rise to particular actions. To say that racism is institutionalized is to say, for instance, that the news media, the education system, the police, the law, are largely complicit in, and function to construct and uphold, racist discourses. Because these discourses are powerful, they are able to influence and dictate actions; quite simply, what we *know* informs what we *do*. Discourse analysis, then, can allow us to examine how particular forms of knowledge come to be, and to study their effects in concrete situations. Discourse analysis entails a close and critical reading of texts, sometimes with detailed attention to such things as word choice, the order of ideas, sentence structure, emphasis, and various other functions of language and expression.[27] A text can be anything composed of language – a conversation, a book, a lecture, an interview – not only a written source. Foucauldian methodology both includes and moves beyond this kind of reading; it is ultimately concerned with the effect of discourse, with *practices* – with what is enacted or produced 'on the ground.' The discourse of 'cultures of poverty,' for example, shaped national welfare policy and was employed by local governments in regulating slum areas in cities. It informed public knowledge about slums. It contributed to the destruction of Africville and other communities.

Culture itself is a significant formulation. Racism's earlier roots in biological explanations have been contested in the twentieth century. While racism may remain fundamentally informed by beliefs in biological difference, it is now more commonly expressed through the language of *cultural* inferiority, and this will be significant in my analysis of Africville's story. Particularly in chapter 3, I explain how culturalized racism figured in Africville with references to theories of 'cultures of poverty' common at the time.

Throughout this work, I also refer to subjectivity or subject position. As social *subjects*, we act as 'characters' who conduct ourselves within the framework of discourses. The character, or subject, is produced through discourses, and is also historically and contextually specific. For example, Foucault examined stock identities such as 'the hysterical woman' of the nineteenth century and 'the madman in the asylum,'[28] much as I identified the 'violent young black man' as a figure – a fiction – that is constructed through current discourse. Bronwyn Davies has argued that to analyse such subjects makes apparent their 'fictionality, whilst recognizing how powerful fictions are in constituting what we take to be real.'[29] The subject is produced in and through discourse, 'gradually, progressively, really and materially constituted through a multiplicity of organisms, forces, energies, materials, desires, thoughts.'[30] What this conceptual framework allows me to do is to imagine social actors operative in the Africville decision as particular kinds of subjects, informed by dominant knowledge about black people, about black spaces, about the slum, and about white dominance. It allows an interrogation of the social and political realities, the discursive and material forces that shape both identities and practices in contextually specific ways.

It is difficult, when evoking subjects, regulation, and power, to avoid 'the body' as a referential point. To evoke the body is a deliberate attempt to understand how physical bodies are objectified, how they are produced in specific ways, how they are understood, 'read,' or inscribed with meaning. It obliges us to consider, to paraphrase Judith Butler, how bodies *matter*.[31] Bodies get sick, they are ugly or beautiful in different cultures and historical eras, they have skin colours, they age, they reproduce. Foucault saw the body as the principal target of power, and incites us to think about how power is enacted specifically, to produce, affect, regulate, and rule individuals. Mainly, two kinds of bodies are produced in Western society: normal bodies and abnormal bodies. Alternatively, we can understand these as 'respectable' and 'degenerate' bodies, both of which are imprinted with particular (differing) gendered, racial, cultural, and other meanings. My theoretical approach employs the body to call attention specifically to the corporeality of how racialized people are marked, managed, observed, and perceived by the dominant group, as well as how the dominant body remains *un*marked. It is intended to signal that racism is *materialized*; it does not simply remain at the level of ideas and ideologies. Violence requires bodies, hunger and poverty are felt in bodies, and exclusion from particular spaces is experienced directly at the individual, physical level. To refer to the physical body is to acknowledge that the practices of colonization, racism, and violence require bodies, not simply people or concepts, in order to realize dominance.[32]

The Terrain of Africville: Race and Space

Decision makers in Africville's story were, directly and indirectly, those who produced studies and reports on the black community. As the following chapters demonstrate, researchers, reporters, and urban planners constructed the official story to be learned and circulated about Africville and about black communities generally. The public received, in their morning papers, depictions of a vile and dangerous place, occupied by ignorant people with strange and revolting habits. They opened their national magazine to learn of a sinister jungle in their midst, in which residents were hostile and ungrateful for efforts to save them. And whether or not all of white Nova Scotia consciously accepted these depictions, they had inherited a history in which racialized segregation and violence were naturalized, one in which the space of the racial Other was seen to await a civilizing, regulatory white footprint.

My references to space, territory, or terrain are never simply figurative. I have noted that space and race are requisite conceptual frameworks for making sense of Africville's destruction. White settlement in Nova Scotia took place within a broader imperial project that included the domination and colonization of native peoples in the quest to overtake their territories. British preoccupation with establishing the British-ness of the new land determined who would end up where, and what they would then be given or permitted to do. In some ways, the technologies by which this spatial management has been maintained over the years have changed little.[33] Even where their specific forms have shifted, the *significance* of space in racial containment has not weakened. To develop this contention in the context of Africville, I draw on theory that makes explicit connections between space and subjectivity. This has entailed an examination of how both dominant and subordinate identities are made through, and come to understand themselves in, distinct spaces. At the same time, space is understood conceptually as a dynamic phenomenon, which influences how and what we come to know about communities and people. To unpack what this means, the discussion must follow several main assertions: First, spaces do not simply predate historical events which occur 'in' them; they develop along with and are shaped by social relations and ideologies. Second, social space plays a role in signifying and enabling certain forms of knowledge production; in turn, such knowledge constitutes space in particular ways. Third, space makes certain kinds of identities possible, both dominant and subordinate, and these groups necessarily inhabit separate spheres. Finally, racialized, spatial separateness and the differential values placed upon people have concrete repercussions in their daily lives. David Goldberg writes of the 'institutional implications of racialized discourse and racist expression for the spatial location and consequent marginalization of groups of people constituted as races.'[34] Similarly, the discourses I consider are not benign forms of 'talk'; they are identified in order to map their spatial implications and effects.

Throughout this work, I often speak of 'racialization' or 'racialized' peoples and spaces. Put simply, to racialize a population is to fashion knowledge about that group with characteristics attributed to its racial origins. But for this to have meaning, 'race' must be already understood to exist as an uncontested category. Racialization as a process thus relies on a notion of race as an 'essential' quality, as something fixed and objective; racial differences must be commonly accepted as evident or 'real.' Conversely, it is now more common to think of race as a destabilized idea, as it is no longer believed to have biological significance. Some social theorists argue that race is not a useful term, or, in fact, that it reinforces older, essentialist racist meanings. Some opt for terms like 'ethnicity' or 'culture' to describe what were once 'racial' categories. The danger in this relabelling is that analysis of the continued power and effect of racial signification is often lost. Race as a concept has long been employed to mark groups as inferior, to rank groups hierarchically, and to set certain groups apart from the dominant society – bodily, spatially, and socially. Such beliefs about race remain deeply entrenched in contemporary societies; they have not been simply abandoned as arbitrary since theories of biological inferiority have been debunked. Further, the social structural effects of such beliefs continue and are not simply undone by changes in attitude or new information. The 'colourblind' approach to racism – 'we are all just the same' – is employed much less as an anti-racist position and more as a denial that race and its consequences continue to profoundly shape individual lives and social relations: if we don't name it, it doesn't exist. Further, this neoconservative notion that race is simply an archaic misconception is often applied for particular political ends – to deny ongoing systemic inequality.

As I employ it, then, race is understood to be a product of ideology, not of biology or observable fact, and its use is intended to signal its ongoing salience as a force in structuring social hierarchies.[35] While it is a historical fiction, it cannot be understood outside the social context and relations through which it arises. To reduce race as a concept even to the status of physical impression is to assume that such impressions are not formed within socially and culturally specific circumstances, as well as at particular times in history. Historian Barbara Fields states, 'Once ideology is stripped away, nothing remains except an abstraction which, while meaningful to a statistician, could scarcely have inspired all the mischief that race has caused during its malevolent historical career.'[36]

Michael Omi and Howard Winant coin the phrase 'racial formation' as 'the sociohistorical process by which racial categories are created, inhabited, transformed, and destroyed.' They write:

> The effort must be made to understand race as an unstable and 'decen-tered' complex of social meanings constantly being transformed by politi-cal struggle. With this in mind, let us propose a definition: *race is a concept which signifies and symbolizes social conflicts and interests by referring to differ-ent types of human bodies* ... Thus we should think of race as an element of social structure rather than as an irregularity within it; we should see race as a dimension of human representation rather than an illusion.[37]

When I refer to groups as racialized, I mean to invoke historically spe-cific understandings that have resulted from political processes – or, the ideology of race that figures in a historical era. What did blackness mean, then, in mid-century Nova Scotia? What set it apart from white-ness? What ideologies informed white understandings of racial differ-ence and why did they matter? Specifically, how did separate social spaces figure in marking different groups? How did the space of Africville, not just physically, but also metaphorically, bolster racial knowledge about its inhabitants?

Racialized spaces are marginal – the project, the ghetto, the reser-vation – and are occupied by groups who are marked as inferior by dominant society. And race as a meaningful category has not always relied on skin colour. Predominantly white spaces may be racialized if they exhibit qualities similar to Other groups or exist in proximity to them. The white working class, the poor, the Irish, white prostitutes, and countless others have been racialized by dominant groups, in some contexts, at some historical moments. Spaces take on racial connotations accordingly. At the same time, a dialectic exists in which space influences social relations, even as it is constituted by them. A good example is Halifax's North End, where 21 per cent of the population was black, according to a 1960s study. This area was labelled pejoratively as 'the negro section,' as if this racial fifth coloured the entire space. While 'negro' is no longer used, 'the North End' continues to connote blackness in Halifax, much like Harlem in New York City or the Jane-Finch corridor in Toronto. Such perceptions infuse space with meanings that have material consequences, such as influencing or limiting the activities of inhabitants, or perpetuating their receipt of inferior services.

A spatial analysis of Africville in relation to the city of Halifax illuminates how white dominance and subjectivity are secured through the incitement to place, replace, and displace people in particular spaces, as well as to make and remake the spaces themselves. Ultimately, this analysis disrupts the common assumption that the relocation program was based on good intentions which simply failed. It does so by insisting that racial discourses and spatial management have always been pervasive and deliberate; they exist at all levels of decision making.

Throughout this book, I employ terms such as *racialization, racial knowledge, racialized groups,* and *racialized spaces* to specify different components or processes of racism. To racialize is to discriminate, to designate a group, or an individual member of a group, as inferior. Such acts are key components of the systemic, institutionalized forms of racism with which I am primarily concerned. This work is a systematic inquiry into discourses, the ideologies they support, and the productive effects of those ideologies, which are concretely lived.

Why Write Something New about Africville?

Standing on Africville's ground on that grey day eight years ago, I knew that even had I been born in Halifax a few decades earlier, I would not have come to Africville. I would have attended high school to hear white boys bragging about their weekend exploits, drinking and driving through Africville in an act of daring defiance, much the way those I knew laughed over their drives into the city and down Hollis Street to see the hookers. These journeys are about race, gender, class, the crossing of boundaries, and the safe return home again. They can be actual or metaphorical, but they always accomplish at least one thing: the creation of a subjectivity through which degenerate spaces can be known, experienced. The space of the Other is available, yet separate, affording one the knowledge that home remains elsewhere, distinct. The dispossession of spaces deemed marginal bolsters the development of 'respectable' white space, and their presence allows the wastes of white space to be housed somewhere else (recall the dumping of night soil/excrement and garbage at Africville's door).

Marginal spaces have everything to do with my history, because they offer the white subject a place to explore, to exploit, to *become*, and, the ultimate choice, to withdraw. And for this reason it is imperative to consider why I am 'here,' whether walking or writing. This consideration is not intended as guilty confession, or as disclosure of my identity in a token bow to political correctness. Rather, it is the product of, and thus serves to illustrate, larger sets of racialized relations that underpin Africville's story. I am not separate from these politics; it matters that the author comes from *somewhere*; it matters that I am, in fact, writing about 'home,' as both inhabitant and intruder.

It also matters in an ethical sense. Academics, perhaps more than others, contributed to the pathologizing of Africville and of black communities generally. The nature of 'study' has been to approach from 'above' as an expert, as one who can know the problem and produce the appropriate diagnosis and treatment. The documentation of racial and cultural difference has often been represented as an objective project, to which the researcher from the dominant group brings no personal history or values. He or she simply collects information about a given population and makes this knowledge available to those in decision-making roles. The media and the education system recycle the information, and purport to convey the facts objectively, while decisions as to which facts are highlighted and how they are portrayed remain unseen. These technologies of knowledge production are rarely made visible in Africville's story. It is one thing to say that many people now recognize that false or problematic knowledge was created and circulated, or that stereotypes proliferated; it is another to critically and conscientiously trace their production, mobilization, and effects. It is one thing to say that many of us now question the integrity of purported liberal justifications for Africville's destruction/integration that were offered at the time; it is another to look closely at the structure and meaning of those discourses, their place in history, and what that might tell us about whiteness, and how processes of racialization play out. This work does not really uncover new data about Africville's history. It rereads what has been said, with a hindsight informed by much critical theory on race, particularly from scholars of colour. In this retelling, I attempt to unearth and develop some of the underlying themes of the relocation decision that have gone largely unconsidered in the white community, the press, and academic scholarship.

I have summarized what I feel are the newer contributions of spatial analysis and knowledge production, yet, there remains something more fundamental that needs to be said. As the subtitle declares, Africville is not about geographies and spaces alone – it is a geography *of racism*. This analysis is what I think of as a 'history in spatial terms' of racism: it maps the formation, transformation, duration, destruction, and commemoration that govern the corporealities of how life can be lived in a space. My work is far from the first or only source to consider Africville's destruction. It is definitely not the only source that is critical of the city government or its policies. Still, as chapter 4 will illustrate, much writing fails to name racism, to locate it in specific institutions or practices, at the core of Africville's destruction. Where some racism in the communities of whites is mentioned, it is rarely located in specific actions or bodies, nor is it seen as a continuous facet of everyday life over time. It is more common to hear of the vaguely 'unfortunate' circumstances of residents, stemming from long-ago discrimination that is not seen to continue. Many sources are critical of the Africville dislocation for its failure to provide adequately for residents or for its lack of follow-up. Some do acknowledge a history of racism that has historically shaped the destinies of black Nova Scotians. However, even when racism is acknowledged, many writers have been hesitant to suggest that it fundamentally determined the Africville decision. Factors such as industrial progress, the development of the slum, and urban renewal, for instance, are presented *along with* the existence of racism, but are not seen to be constituted by it. Poverty is often the focus of discussion about Africville's problems, while racism is seen to have *contributed* to poverty, rather than to be intimately bound up with it in a very present and ongoing way.

In much research on Africville, authors tread lightly over racism; they take pains to make clear that none of the decision makers intended any harm. While this may be true, the result is a disembodied, amorphous racism that simply 'occurs,' like a natural disaster far in the past. We cannot seriously consider the operation of racism unless it can be located in specific practices and sites. When it remains a 'free-floating' concept, relegated to 'history,' there are no implicated parties, no conscious decisions, and there is no harm. This is not to suggest that individuals or groups were always fully aware of the consequences of their decisions; but it is to assert that researchers and decision makers operated within a context of racism that had been so firmly in place for centuries as to make it quite natural, and thus invisible, to them.

At the same time that I question assertions of an unqualified positive intent to desegregate Halifax and to improve the lives of Africville people, I also acknowledge that discursive and spatial practices have far-reaching effects which cannot always be predicted. There is no simple dichotomy between 'good' and 'bad' intentions. Thus I am not suggesting that researchers or officials in the Africville decision operated out of *bad* intent, but rather that the unrelenting insistence on their *good* intent, at the time of forced relocation as well as in the present, diverts serious consideration of the consequences and harm in their actions. I suggest that the emphasis on benevolence must be tabled and that investments in innocence must be relinquished, in order to analyse how, regardless of what decision makers thought they were doing, they did it in a specific context, fuelled by racist ideology.

While many factors, rather than a singular 'cause,' influenced the destruction of Africville, what is often missed is how the various factors supported one another. For example, racialization *and* urban renewal *and* white paternalism occur in concert, as inseparable factors. But is urban renewal not itself about racism? Is the failure to consult with Africville residents simply an oversight, or is it the product of racism? Is it even an oversight, or is it a necessity? A critical race analysis, then, emerges through the interlocking understanding of racial discourse, spatial regulation, social restructuring, and all their concomitant epistemologies, *as they constitute one another.*

What Follows

This chapter has sought to introduce the historical context, the key questions to be explored, and some basic theoretical foundations, and to situate and problematize the author and authorship itself. What remains are four interlinked discussions that elucidate the story's fundamental elements – the construction, denigration, destruction, and commemoration of Africville.

The next chapter offers a theoretical framework for examining the story. This framework examines how dominant groups mark others as racially inferior, and regulate their communities and lives, through the control of space. To understand how both racialized and dominant subjects are made, and how racism is realized and enacted, we must attend to the significance of space in social life. The discussion questions common understandings of space as simply a passive or 'empty' ground upon which events occur. Rather, space, or place, matters; it affects patterns of settlement, the drawing of boundaries, access to resources, and how we understand differences among groups. I explore the connections between subjects, identity, spaces, and power, to understand how 'the slum,' as a concept, developed and gained meaning in Africville's case. At the same time, through examples from the work of social geographers, I attempt to assert the concrete, lived effects of racism on people and places, and their endurance and reification over time.

Chapter 3 moves to a more specific reading of my research context – examining the racial discourses that were created and propagated by white planners, city officials, researchers, the media and other professionals about black communities during the mid-twentieth century in Nova Scotia. These discourses are significant as they form the dominant body of knowledge around which decisions about Africville's future came to be made. They illustrate the construction of black communities as 'separate' and excluded from normative understandings of civility and development, and they explain dominant perceptions of deviant, impoverished, racialized 'cultures.' They include characteristics of the racial urban slum and the coinciding values and practices of the people who live there. This discussion draws on prominent texts and news reports of the time to relay the modes of study, observation, and regulation of the racial Other that prevailed. In this chapter I attempt to understand how knowledge and power are related, how knowledge feeds the capacity to govern, making certain actions possible.

This discussion sets the context for a 'spatial' walk, in chapter 4, through the same terrain. Here, it is clearer that more than one kind of subjectivity is made in racialized space: dominant subjects require subordinates, and dominant identities are made through encounter and negotiation with difference as much as through exclusion. This analysis brings together the spatial theory and the racial discourses explored so far to illustrate how Africville was destroyed. Projects of erasure, I argue, are ongoing; they adopt different forms over time, stretching into the present day. This process is not unique to Africville; rather, Africville is but one site at which to read the broader interlocking narratives of race, space, and subjectivity. It is my contention that racism was the fundamental reason for the dislocation of Africville people from their community. However, this cannot be simply explained as a direct translation of conscious attitude into action. It was, rather, a deliberate expulsion based on notions of order and progress that could not accommodate the radical Otherness black communities were thought to embody. It was explained through white-defined desires for integration that were seen to preclude racist views. Race, then, is often coded in the language that authors employ to study and consider Africville's fate; the dominant discourses they access to explain what was done claim an *anti*-racist stance that is seen as axiomatic in the goal of integration. In addition, writers and officials often explain the relocation program's failure as a product of historical neglect or an unfortunate outcome, despite good intent. I reject this explanation, arguing that racist narratives are so firmly entrenched in systemic modes of knowledge and governance that such an interpretation is naive. While emphasizing that racism is systemic, I also pay attention to the words and actions of individuals, who, I argue, learn, act, and operate within these systems. It is often in the details of day-to-day talk and interaction that we best see how the destruction unfolds.

The final chapter carries the study of spatial regulation into the present day by examining the commemoration of Africville. Here, I posit that whites continue to manage the space of Africville in specific ways. These have included the suppression of protest, the dismissing of harm to the black community, and the continued support for an 'official story' of progress and integration that obscures past actions. Further, this chapter discusses how the construction of present-day knowledge about Africville relies on the alteration and control of the landscape. The continuing story is that of an ongoing, symbolic eviction of Africville from its own space. I examine this through official responses of whites to ongoing protests by Africville people and their descendants, whose expulsion they have not yet acknowledged or compensated.

Implicit throughout my project is the struggle to understand how 'we,' as white subjects, come to grapple with and make sense of histories of racism and, in particular, with violent acts that exemplify and punctuate these histories. And I say 'we' with a grain of salt – intending not to alienate non-white readers, but to be clear that it is whites who must come to terms with these events and histories in particular ways – not through paralysing guilt or defensive denial, but as accountable subjects who *benefit* from racism. I do not proclaim any correct or conclusive ways to do this; I do not claim to know what those ways might entail. This story is one contribution to a dialogue about innocence and accountability, and how we might start to think about racism in such a way that it is not simply someone else's problem. Africville has become a symbol, for local blacks, of community, resistance, and strength. What is Africville to whites? It is to this question that this book is ultimately addressed.

2 Placing Africville:
The Making of the Slum

At some very basic level, imperialism means thinking about, settling on, controlling land that you do not possess, that is distant, that is lived on and owned by others. For all kinds of reasons it attracts some people and often involves untold misery for others.

Edward Said[1]

Dominant groups, such as colonizers, have always defined, confined, regulated, and eradicated groups marked as racially inferior through the control of space. Dominant groups express their own identities, and reinforce what they see as their rightful rule, through acts of regulation and destruction of the racial Other – and, simultaneously, through space. There are many discourses that feed and justify these acts of racism; these specific formulations of racial knowledge are the subject of the next chapter. For now, to put it simply, it matters not only that these acts take place, but *where* they take place.

Why think about space? What is necessary to understand about space, in order to understand what was done to Africville? It is not that a spatial analysis is the only way to look at things, or that its absence would invalidate another kind of take on how racialization happens. However, when I began to think about Africville and visited its former site, it struck me that at a basic level, Africville's establishment and eradication is all about territory. It is about white people's self-proclaimed right to land that was not theirs.

I am a sociologist, not a geographer. I note the risks of delving into an unfamiliar field, and know that my appreciation of the body of geographic work on space is bound to be limited. But I join other social theorists in what has become a compelling transdisciplinary incitement to understand how geographic configurations inform historical and social processes.

In this chapter I engage a number of theorists who endeavour to understand what space means in social histories. This is not a comprehensive exploration of the literature, but a selection of work that covers a range of historical analyses and that deals with central concepts that have helped me to think about Africville in spatial terms. Many of the sources engaged here analyse late-eighteenth- and nineteenth-century European and colonial spatial arrangements. This is significant and appropriate as it matches the time period in which Nova Scotia's population was suddenly quadrupled (with the arrival of the Loyalists in the 1780s), and that of the ensuing decades during which British norms and values anchored the new society. The spatial relations in Halifax today are the legacy of arrangements that have been central, all along, to the building of the city as a white space.

I also draw on twentieth-century theory about slum administration to show how technologies of spatial management continue into the period of Africville's destruction and beyond. By the book's final chapter, it is apparent how, at the commemorative stage of Africville's history, even while they have shifted to address new concerns, spatialized forms of racism remain entrenched.

Space

We often perceive places to be naturally occurring, to have simply emerged and developed over time. To trace the historical events, policies, relations, and struggles that have made them as they are is to reveal that spaces are socially produced, whether the results of comprehensive planning or of indifferent neglect. Henri Lefebvre writes:

> Space is not a scientific object removed from ideology and politics; it has always been political and strategic. If space has an air of neutrality and indifference with regard to its contents ... it is precisely because it has been occupied and used, and has already been the focus of past processes whose traces are not always evident on the landscape. Space has been shaped and molded from historical and natural elements, but this has always been a political process ... It is a product literally filled with ideologies.[2]

Concrete, physical processes, then, determine the nature of space, its content, and how life is lived within it. But space also has metaphorical significance. We attach meanings and judgments to spaces and those who inhabit them – we think differently about members of an old, established wealthy neighbourhood than about a group of recent immigrants living in an urban ghetto. Spaces themselves influence how their occupants know themselves, and how they are known by outsiders, although such a relationship has not always been explicit in social analysis.

Lefebvre is best remembered for his critique of two traditional strains of geographic inquiry. On the one hand, geographers saw space as a fixed and empty 'slate' on which social history was written. Alternatively, space was seen as *only* an end result of social processes, and these processes were not themselves 'placed' in particular sites that would influence their outcome. In both instances, space is left in a passive role, insignificant in determining human relations.

Lefebvre, and others in his wake, argued that a dialectical model is more apt. In this, the particular form spaces take is seen as a result of historical developments and processes. At the same time, space itself matters; it influences the relations and processes that can take place within it. Space is not only a mirror of social actions, but space and the processes of social life are dynamic; they reinforce one another.[3] As Edward Soja describes: 'Spatiality situates social life in an active arena where purposeful human agency jostles problematically with tendential social determinations to shape everyday activity, particularise social change, and etch into place the course of time and the making of history.'[4] This acknowledgment of the tension between agency and determinants beyond our control provides a foundation for thinking about the various entry points from which people create, live in, react to, and are affected by spaces.

Lefebvre defined three distinct forms of space: 'Perceived' space refers to the daily activities and practices of life that occur in particular places, as well as how space organizes the activities that can and cannot take place within it. It is often thought of as 'real' space. 'Conceived' space refers to conceptions of space from outside. It is commonly thought of as 'imagined' – for instance, by those designing a place and determining its function in society. Third, in 'lived' space, both perceived and conceived space are reconfigured and represented by the space's occupants. The linking of representational or metaphoric aspects of space with the physical spaces of people's lives is theorized by Eugene McCann. Lefebvre's theory, he notes, is applicable precisely because it is rooted in everyday life practices in space.[5]

Soja, too, has insisted on the study of spaces for both their materiality and their representational, or symbolic elements at once. He defines a 'thirdspace' in which these interconnected elements can be read simultaneously, and which accounts for the agency of residents in embodying their space in particular ways – often strategic and innovative.[6] It is unlikely, for instance, that most residents of Africville saw it as a segregated community, and why would they? They did not design their space to exclude non-black residents (nor did this occur).[7] Rather, their pattern of settlement was shaped by historical solidarity, migratory cohesiveness, the need to share resources and information, common religious and community values, and the need for a refuge from discrimination.

Segregated arrangements often function positively to maintain stability and survival in communities.[8] As pointed out by bell hooks, in particular, communities occupying marginal space have a potentially clear vantage point on the dominant society's motives and actions.[9] While the margin is often thought of as a site to which socially underprivileged groups are *relegated*, theorists, such as Lefebvre (in the notion of lived space), Soja (in *Thirdspace*) and hooks, reposition the margin as a potentially empowering locale from which groups and individuals are able to enact resistance. Of course, these situations must be considered within the broader political and social contexts that restrict residents' choices, as it is the very fact of marginalization in the first place that necessitates strategic resistance.[10] As Steven Gregory makes clear, the negotiations of black community identity, resistance, and life struggles are more complex than is often apparent. They encompass an entangled web of factors, both internal and external to a community, and always rooted in history, social policy, and economic interests, that shape a community's settlement patterns and its desire and ability to reshape them.[11]

My foci of analysis in this work are the processes of spatial segregation and governance that are imposed by dominant actors, and, as will be seen, the processes of *desegregation* that are imposed as 'solutions' to the problems of the poor and racialized. Thus, while it is important to keep in mind the agency of marginalized groups, it is this dominant vantage point that is the central object of my critique.

Space, Identity, and Power

There is a dynamic relationship between space and subjects: we understand who we are according to the place we inhabit; the place we inhabit, in part, determines who we can be. This becomes apparent in pejorative depictions of 'slum' residents (by researchers, journalists, or others) that are based on the condition of their surroundings, while at the same time, the space of the slum itself is seen to have become what it is due to their occupation. To read the slum as a representational or 'third' space is to pay attention to its perceived, conceived, and lived elements at once. How do people occupy the slum? What are they enabled to do within it? What does it mean to them, and how do they understand their home and themselves? At the same time, how do others understand the slum; how do they set out to place it in particular ways, to form it through design or policy, to change it over time? What does the slum make apparent about spaces outside it, spaces that are different and separate? What does it reflect about dominant society? Through such questions, we begin to form a methodology that encompasses various meanings, lived and metaphoric.

Michel Foucault also believed that spaces were significant in ordering social life, particularly as vehicles for forging control over the body, or the physicality of life. His work is replete with spatial metaphors and architectural references about the forms of spaces that made surveillance, control, and self-regulation possible. He also made explicit his concern with spaces where populations deemed deviant were confined. In the concept of 'biopower,' he defined a specifically middle class European preoccupation, since the seventeeth century, with regulating the processes of life. Biopower is concerned with the protection of life through regulation of health, reproduction, death, the body, the family, and other biological phenomena (as opposed to ideological or political concerns). Biopower arose in contrast to earlier forms of sovereign power, under which the sovereign was obeyed, defended, and possessed the right to take life. Biopower is expressed through the right of the 'social body' as a whole to live and to reproduce itself. Subjects engage in microprocesses of regulating the functions of life – birth and death rates, housing, immigration patterns, and so on. In Foucault's words, the emergence of biopower entailed 'an explosion of numerous and diverse techniques for achieving the subjugation of bodies and the control of populations.'[12]

Following the logic of biopower, dominant groups assert that those deemed degenerate must die (not always literally, but they must be removed or subjugated at some level) in order that the mainstream social body can continue to live. This necessitates the physical separation and confinement of populations deemed unfit for habitation in dominant society – not, primarily, as a means of punishment, but as a means of moral discipline. Bodies require prohibitions and restraints, and unruly (ill, insane, criminal, racialized) bodies require specific techniques of policing, confinement, and regulation. The goal of such disciplinary power is 'not only that bodies should do what one wishes, but that they should *operate* as one wishes.'[13] In other words, discipline ignites an effective ongoing self-regulation. It does not simply command one to behave in a particular way, rather, the required behaviour becomes desirable to the population over time, and is self-perpetuating. Discipline produces 'subjected' bodies, subjects that can be governed. Foucault's historical work attended to the specific spaces where the confinement and discipline of groups are accomplished – the prison, the school, the asylum.

Such an analysis has implications for marginalized people of colour in particular city neighbourhoods, slums, or housing developments. In Foucault's later work, he specifically links biopower to state racism, which he sees as a basic, potential mechanism of this regulatory power.[14] Racism functions to delineate, separate, and, ultimately, to eliminate groups that are seen as a threat to the social body at the level of *life*. Racism serves to justify the spatial segregation, and the eradication, of populations that are seen to impede survival and development of the population or the race. In effect, this means that the taking of life is justifiable when it is committed for the good of the social body. Drawing on Foucault's theory, Eduardo Mendieta writes, 'Racism, in short, is an expression of a new form of power, a power that is both individualizing and generalizing, a power that acts on the individual by acting on a people as if it were a living entity.' He concludes that 'racism is biopolitic's war on the body politic for the sake of its life.'[15]

When read against notions of progress and modern urban growth in its particular time frame, Africville is illuminated as a space that the city sought to control and demolish. Even in their eventual eviction and dispersal, Africville residents remained a threat to the social body. Racialized groups are seen not only to live within defiled spaces, but to embody those spaces.

In essence, it is the conceptual tools offered by spatial theory that make a difference in how we think about space and Africville. This means remembering to think beyond 'space as container' or 'space as the end result of history,' and to ask different questions – not just, How do communities come to be slums? but also, What does the slum *mean*, what does it represent, in the imagination of those who live elsewhere? and How does the community known as a slum matter to those who do live there? Further, it means keeping in mind the dynamic relationship between space and subjects: What do we know about certain kinds of people because of the spaces they occupy? and What do we do as a result of this knowledge (i.e. avoid them, closely document their behaviours, create laws to remove them)?

Where these kinds of questions come to life is in specific empirical examples. In the rest of this chapter, I outline sources that enable me to think about various types of spatial arrangements and codings – those that are made through colonization, in urban development, in the middle class home, and in the slum itself. Spatial arrangements and their negotiation by subjects in different ways are enlightening for a study of racism. The central concern is: How do we use theories of space in order to make sense of racialized bodies, colonial conquest, the development of the modern city in racial terms, the slum, forced relocation programs, and modern-day modes of public commemoration?

Colonial Subjects and Spaces

> The explorers wish to influence and possess the world they meet, but take great pains to be sure that it will not substantially inform them in return. They evacuate the others they meet, keeping their own subject position in the form of the already formulated, complete monad ... The European explorers attempted to maintain the environment on the 'outside' in order to preserve their mastery of it ... Mapping acted to distinguish 'self' from 'other': in early America, cartography was the measure between human and non-human, civilized and savage ... The solid lines that cartography draws between the subject and the land also reinforce the lines drawn between European white subjects and Others.
>
> Kathleen Kirby[16]

There are various ways to draw lines between people and groups; such lines make clear who belongs where, and what the differences look like. It is in the very act of drawing those lines that dominance is made. The subject who can determine where the line should be and carry out the delineation is the subject who occupies, knows, and owns the territories in question. Various theorists have illustrated these technologies of colonization with reference to the significance of space. As Jane Jacobs has stated, 'The role of the spatial imaginary in the imperial project is perhaps most clearly evident in the spatial practices of mapping and naming.'[17] Further, the mapping and naming in question are never simply benign or 'real' representations of the world; they are political, and situated; they attempt to make strange lands familiar. In so doing, they set the terms by which categories of race, gender, and class have meaning. As Audrey Kobayashi and Linda Peake make clear, the discipline of geography and its practice have served to naturalize the differences these categories seem to embody.[18] The capacity to know the racial Other is the capacity to govern, and this is apparent in many forms throughout the establishment of empire, nation, city, and slum.

Kathleen Kirby examines the mapping of space as fundamental to the formation of the 'cartesian subject,'[19] who explores, conquers, and reformulates space into something felt to be his own. This subject calls to mind conceptualizations of space as inert and unchanging, like those Lefebvre critiques. Similarly, Nicholas Blomley analyses the British preoccupation with carrying out accurate surveys in the New World as a means of documenting and organizing the settlement of the land and of appropriating it from Native peoples. Further, he writes, 'the survey served more than instrumental ends. It arbitrated between an acknowledged regime and those forms of property deemed to lie "outside" the frontier.'[20]

Explorer narratives can offer useful starting points for understanding the gaze of the dominant subject upon the subjugated. Read critically, they illuminate the politics of observation and position mapping as more than simply curiosity or documentation. Mary Louise Pratt has described the growth of a 'planetary consciousness' in the eighteenth century, which involved the intensive study of the earth by European explorers. She finds descriptive works in many sites, such as botanical treatises, naturalist texts, and narrative travel accounts, which were profoundly concerned with the documentation of all components of the natural environment. She too has contended that naturalists' and cartographers' mapping of the world's borders served to bring the Empire and its vast outer reaches into the public European consciousness as a known space, with known contents. Pratt posits the subject of these landscape discourses as the '"seeing man" ... whose imperial eyes passively look out and possess.'[21] Such observation is not, of course, passive. The act of possession secured through mapping is the result of particular ways of knowing and learning about spaces. As Patrick Joyce illustrates in intricate detail, colonial projects of mapping were always motivated by the need to render spaces *governable*. Maps, therefore, did not simply document or reflect spaces, they constructed them as objects of rule. Drawing on Foucault, Joyce is concerned with the modes of knowing that are enabled by surveillance and mapping, as well as with the subject who can know the Other. He writes: 'The abstract, and gendered, gaze of the map was literally superior: the view above was detached, part of a visual rhetoric of modernity which privileged the observer with a vantage point separate from the observed.'[22] Examining the colonial mapping of nations such as Ireland and India, Joyce points to the necessary rationalization of space that underpins the cartographic project.

Space itself can be known, documented, and desired. But, as Edward Said has noted, a central problem for dominant subjects wishing to take over land is the very existence of people;[23] something must be done about the occupants of a land, whether they are placed on reserves, killed, enslaved, or employed as servants. Dara Culhane, citing the concept of *terra nullius* (empty land) in her study of Canadian settlement, shows how inhabited spaces 'were simply legally *deemed to be uninhabited* if the people were not Christian, not agricultural, not commercial, not "sufficiently evolved" or simply in the way.'[24] The legal assignment of space as empty allows a degree of certitude with which occupation can proceed unimpeded.[25] It does not, however, eradicate the problem of actual, remaining bodies, which the colonizer must confront in some way. It is in the proximity of difference that space takes on very specific importance, because once the Other is no longer far away or imagined, new lines must be drawn if we are to be clear about the categories of ruler and ruled.

This is not to say that subjects come to be simply in dichotomous relation to one another – the positions of colonizer and native are not strictly opposites, nor do people embody them in wholly conscious ways. Rather, identity is negotiated in relation with the other, over time. Pratt defines a 'contact zone' in which the complex struggle over identity – who is able to be whom – takes place. She demonstrates how, in the space of cohabitation after invasion by Europeans, power relations could not be adequately described simply through inclusion and exclusion. 'A contact perspective emphasizes how subjects are constituted in and by their relations to each other. It treats the relations between colonizers and colonized, or travelers and "travelees," not in terms of separateness or apartheid, but in terms of copresence, interaction, interlocking understandings and practices, often within radically asymmetrical relations of power.'[26]

Not only are such relations about race and the boundaried realms of colonizer and colonized, but they rely on the interlocking meanings and values attached to gender, sexuality, and middle class family life. Feminist geographers have long been concerned with how gender identities are produced through the separate social realms of public and private. Work focused on the modern city has been particularly interested in the production of public space as a male venue, and with the systemic confinement of women to the middle class home and suburb.[27] However, theories of the public/private split have often been most relevant to white, middle class women, and analyses of gendered spatiality have seen important shifts in the last two decades; Gloria Anzaldua, Chandra Talpade Mohanty,[28] and others have theorized global migrations and the political convergence of different societies across borders, asking how such politics configure women's experiences differently, and in relation to other women.[29] The spatial modes through which feminist analysis is articulated have become more varied. As Alison Blunt and Gillian Rose write, in their introduction to *Writing Women and Space*, feminist geographers have begun to depict how 'different epistemological claims about women's identity produce different interpretations of space itself.'[30]

Racialized bodies do take on particular significance according to gender. But meanings around gender are always about race and always infused with assumptions about socio-economic status or class. Ann Stoler emphasizes the historical specificity of such meanings to the analysis of different colonial contexts. In her work on European colonies, she illustrates that particular politics of sexual intimacy were inextricably linked to matters of state governance. The regulation of sexual relations provided an apparatus by which dominant and subjugated could be distinguished from one another; everyday domestic arrangements consistently called for vigilance around racial mixing.[31] She writes, 'strategies of identity-making and self-affirmation were unstable and in flux. European identities in the colonies were affirmed by a cultural repertoire of competencies and sexual prescriptions that altered with the strategies for profit and the stability of rule.'[32]

A recurrent theme in post-colonial work on space is that intimate and domestic matters serve as microcosms of state concerns – and, more than this, as mechanisms through which state concerns are realized. This is often expressed by feminists who examine the mutual constitution of femininity and racial domination. For instance, Mary-Louise Fellows and Sherene Razack explore the nineteenth-century domestic and economic arrangements through which different categories of women, as subjects, came to be. In doing so, they attend to what are inscribed as feminine spaces and activities, to the daily practices that define and categorize people differently. They write, 'Ladies ... pursued respectability by distancing themselves from dirt and degradation. That distancing could occur neither in the lady's imagination nor in her middle-class home without the economic and sexual exploitation of domestic workers and prostituted women.'[33] Defiled women, then, are relegated not only to social spaces but to particular duties, through which they can be understood as physically and metaphorically different. Razack situates the prostitute as the embodiment of defiled female sexuality, and also notes how such women have been historically racialized.[34] The spatial separation of the zone of prostitution helps to solidify this sense of Otherness. As Evelyn Brooks Higginbotham writes:

> Ladies were not merely women; they represented a class, a differentiated status within the generic category of 'women'. Nor did society confer such status on all white women. White prostitutes, along with many working-class white women, fell outside its rubric. But no black woman, regardless of income, education, refinement or character, enjoyed the status of lady.[35]

As middle-class white women have historically relied on the domestic service of women of colour,[36] they have come to know themselves not simply as superior but as *different kinds of women*.[37]

The insertion of Other bodies into respectable spaces is necessary for the operation of middle class life, yet their presence is problematic and calls for the careful marking of difference. Thus, the bourgeois family allows the 'outside in' for the performance of specific roles. Dirt is exchanged for cleanliness; the duties performed by racialized subjects result in the dirt being, as Razack and Fellows note, 'absorbed' into the bodies of the Other. Dirt is taken away with the racial Other. Excrement is dumped near his water supply; garbage is carted to her backyard. It is through those who fulfil such duties that the dominant subject gains meaning, both materially and symbolically. The spaces of the slum, the field, the factory, or the red-light district make possible the spaces of the bourgeois home and neighbourhood. Yet, it is not simply space that is produced. As we have seen, the women themselves, or the subjects of 'lady' and 'prostitute,' acquire meaning in social space. Meanings of masculinity also figure prominently. Consistent with many of the assumed attributions of the slum itself are racialized depictions of the black male as dangerous and violent.[38] In the twentieth century's shift from biological racism to that justified by 'cultural pathology,'[39] the slum and the ghetto form the terrain on which the criminality of black males is unleashed.

These subjectivities are inscribed on particular bodies, for it is the body that signifies visually, the body that endures violence, and is targeted by racism. These corporeal effects make racism an *experience*, not just a phenomenon.

The Body, Race, and Culture

> Racism is about how one can and cannot be in a body.
> Eduardo Mendieta[40]

Through the relations of colonial rule we are offered various figures – the seeing man, the lady, the cartesian subject. All are situated in spaces, and also in relation to other objectified and subjugated bodies. Such subjects come to be as spatialized figures that can be understood through not only the places they occupy but the places from which they are barred. Several scholars provide excellent examples of this from different settings.

Rhadika Mohanram, in 'Black Body,' traces how black female bodies in the West signify meaning that is articulated through space. The dominant subject, she notes, reads such bodies as rooted to Other places, apart from dominant, respectable space, while whiteness remains unmarked. More than this, elite whiteness entitles one to a freedom of movement, rather than confinement to particular places.[41] Sara Ahmed draws on similar concepts to examine strangeness. She theorizes how bodies are constituted as Other specifically when they are 'out of place' in neighbourhoods or nations. She notes that dominant communities come to know themselves through the Other or the space outside, and that, 'strange bodies are precisely those bodies that are temporarily assimilated *as* the unknown within the encounter: they function as the border that defines both the space into which the familiar body … cannot cross, and the space in which such a body constitutes itself as at home.'[42]

In various contexts, the subjugated, racialized body is rendered 'outside' legitimate space; its movement is dictated by the tacit rights of occupancy. It cannot simply 'be.' For the purposes of my analysis, this notion is especially informative. It speaks to the making of dominant subjects in spatial terms, and it becomes clearer how differently marked subjects take on their disparate meanings through their occupancy of, and ability to enter, particular places. Bodies must be read against the backdrop of their geographies, to understand who is subjugated and who is elite. Further to this, as Puwar Nirmal makes clear, dominant bodies are seen to belong, naturally, to dominant spaces, while others, such as racialized persons and women, are marked as illegitimate 'invaders.'[43] Similarly, Evelyn Peters has critiqued the representation of First Nations peoples as antithetical to urban life. Relegated to reserves, they become symbolically, inextricably linked to these outside spaces, and associated with 'natural' settings that are seen to be congruent with essentialist notions of their cultures.[44] Kathi Wilson and Evelyn Peters describe how the occupation of urban space by First Nations migrants constitutes a disruption of the city's boundaries, as well as a challenge to the notion that all non-reserve land naturally belongs to settlers.[45]

The drawing of spatial boundaries need not be explicit, as it is, for instance, during legal apartheid regimes; the drawing can be tacit, emerging through various forms of public knowledge and discourse, and through institutionalized practices that normalize the occupation of space by a white, dominant figure. Thus, even while marginalized groups are, presumably, 'allowed in,' their proximity constitutes a new problem – the mixing of different bodies in common space begs new forms of delineation. Samira Kawash illustrates this through her analysis of the homeless body in public parks. Through the homeless, she argues, we come to understand who is a legitimate citizen, and who is not. This is realized in the regulation of public places so that the homeless body is consistently evicted from them, while privileged and normalized 'real citizens' are maintained both as their legitimate occupants and those able to govern their use. In essence, the degenerate body – homeless, black, poor, female, or Other – is produced and reproduced through practices of exclusion. A garbage dump is moved to a community; the community's residents are then said to be slum-dwellers, unclean, scavengers. The conditions under which such associations come to be drawn fade quickly and the resulting social ills merely reinforce dominant knowledge of the Other. This is a common thread that runs through my concern with city space, the regulation of slums and racialized ghettoes, and, eventually, the design of commemorative space.

Along the same lines, broader, transnational meanings are imprinted on the racialized body. Edward Said, in *Orientalism*, examines how discourses of the West as enlightened, progressive, and civilized rely on the construction of an imagined, inferior Middle East. The Orient, as barbaric and uncivilized Other, forms a requisite backdrop against which Western culture defines itself. Such an imagined Orient, along with contingent discourses about the Otherness of its space and people, is meaningful in the West insofar as it forms the antithesis of Western civilization and rationality.[46] Similarly, as I suggest in this work, the shadow of Africa as a dangerous, exotic, and untamed land can be seen in various discourses about the black population in Halifax. It is not only within urban space, but also at the level of national belonging, that racialized meanings inform the insider/outsider distinction.

Racing the Slum

Slums, ghettoes, or projects within cities mean many things to those who plan, study, or observe them. Whether they are physically visible or simply known by reputation, multiple negative meanings are attached to them by those who live elsewhere. Due to systemic poverty, and often to the policies and practices of local governments, such spaces often appear, and eventually become, unsafe, unclean, and associated with disease, moral deficiency, and crime. As was the case with Africville, they may be treated as repositories for the wastes of the dominant society or for groups deemed contaminated. The slum is known to be spatially distinct. The borders around it provide both a real and metaphorical distance for those from more privileged classes, most of whom are not racialized in the view of the dominant society. The preservation of respectable spaces relies on the containment of slum conditions in a separate sphere, understood to be 'outside' and beyond the bounds of legitimate society, a space apart, where the rules and conditions of dominant space no longer apply.

David Goldberg traces the technologies of spatial management throughout the colonial and postcolonial eras, delineating a shift from colonial to slum administration in the mid-twentieth century. Consistently, the existence and movement of racially defined populations are seen to create the demand for new modes of maintaining spatial boundaries. As Culhane reminds us through the concept of *terra nullius*, Europeans who colonized the Americas envisioned the vast tracts of land as 'empty.' They imagined uncolonized spaces to be devoid of human habitation, seeing the indigenous populations they encountered as inferior at best, subhuman at worst. With the later flow of formerly colonized people into the cities of North America and Europe, stricter arrangements had to be configured and maintained to keep the racial Other spatially and metaphorically distant from the privileged classes. Proximity instates a whole new level of concern. Faced with what Barnor Hesse calls the 'internal Other,' as opposed to the colonized Other overseas, colonial management saw a need for the 'rationalization of city space,'[47] which resulted in the growth of poor racialized areas and a host of accompanying discourses about the nature of these spaces and their residents.

Patrick Joyce, in his work on the cartographic gaze, traces mapping into the nineteenth century, noting its most profound effect on the 'city centre dwellings of the poor,' which 'were understood to breed both immorality and ill-health.'[48] Discourses of crime, moral degeneracy, filth, and general ineptitude act in concert with spatial restrictions, both justifying and reifying them. Hesse describes this process as 'a spatial nativization in which people are compressed into prefabricated landscapes, the ghetto, the shanty town, and undergo a process of "representational essentializing" ... in which one part or aspect of people's lives comes to epitomize them as a whole.'[49]

Of course, such developments are much more than matters of representation or figurative prejudice. They stem from violent histories and they function in violent ways. Representation is more than merely words. It is discourses and images that are mutually constitutive of policies and practices, whose effects are concretely lived. Due to substandard resources allotted racialized ghettos, as well as the original poverty of immigrants who inhabited them, conditions in these neighbourhoods rapidly decline. As Peter Marcuse explains through the concept of the 'residual city,' racial minority spaces frequently came to house the wastes of society, pollutants from industrial manufacturing, sewer systems and garbage disposal areas, or housing for others deemed undesirable, such as patients with infectious diseases or homeless people.[50] Even where such conditions are attributed in lip service to governmental policy, (as they sometimes were in Africville), they are ultimately bound up in racial discourses that tie the filth, disease, and disorder to the bodies of inhabitants of the slum. Peter Stallybrass and Allon White discuss this phenomenon in their work on the evolution of the nineteenth century slum:

> the metonymic associations (between the poor and animals, between the slum-dweller and sewage) are read at first as the signs of an imposed social condition for which the State is responsible. But the metonymic associations (which trace the *social* articulation of 'depravity') are constantly elided with and displaced by a metaphoric language in which filth stands in for the slum-dweller: the poor *are* pigs.[51]

This dehumanization coincides with a sense of moral outrage on behalf of the upper classes that the poor, in their unclean and disorderly habits, may transgress the boundaries of 'civilized' areas.[52] David Goldberg also writes of the conflation of physical conditions with immorality, adding that racial dehumanization further infuses such representations.

> The slum is by definition filthy, foul smelling, wretched, rancorous, uncultivated, and lacking care. The *racial* slum is doubly determined, for the metaphorical stigma of a black blotch on the cityscape bears the added connotations of moral degeneracy, natural inferiority, and repulsiveness ... the slum locates the lower class, the racial slum the *under*class.[53]

Goldberg delineates displacement from the rest of society as 'the primary mode by which the space of racial marginality has been articulated and reproduced.'[54] Such displacement is further reinforced through references to the racial origins of inhabitants that become embedded in discourse about any space they occupy. For example, the terms 'Chinatown' and 'Africville' were reclaimed by their occupants, but were originally racial markers attributed from outside the communities to signify their essential difference. The separateness connoted in a word comes to stand in for and capture a collection of racist narratives, whether they depict an exotic Far East or a 'dark continent' of savages. As Kay Anderson demonstrates in her study of Chinatown, white public discourses portrayed residents as the embodiment of all the negative qualities and activities associated with their homelands, including the opium trade, white slavery, and prostitution. Chinatown, she argues, was seen as an essential micro-representation of 'Chinese-ness' in the West. Its spatial containment, through different techniques and according to different social requirements over time, illuminates much about white society, which came to know its dominance through this necessary Other space. Chinatown was depicted in the media as filthy, morally repugnant, and presenting a great danger to the rest of society – images that consistently relied on stereotypes of the Far East.[55] Stallybrass and White's inquiry, too, reveals depictions of Britain's poor that are never *only* about class. They found that the Irish in England were racialized as barbaric and animalistic, and that slum areas were frequently compared to the colonized lands in Africa as the city's 'dark places.'

Such images, as can be seen in historical, moral readings of the slum, also rely on gender and sexual norms and how they shape family and community. Anderson notes, of Chinatown:

> racist knowledges had gender and moral codings relating to family, sexuality, marriage and residence embedded within them, just as discourses surrounding gender, sex, citizenship and family life relied on race meanings for their cultural integrity. It follows that race identities cannot be decontextualized and separated off analytically or politically from the constitution of other identities and axes of power.[56]

In the descriptive literature on black Nova Scotian communities, which I discuss in the next chapter, such factors are extensively documented. Discourses of slum removal make explicit moral assumptions as to how family arrangements and parenting styles hinder the development of children, the safety of neighbourhoods, and the overall potential for cleanliness, order, and respectability. Racialization could not be accomplished in the absence of particular definitions of masculinity, femininity, family, and community.

Contamination, Containment, and Transgression

White European beliefs in the inherent dangers and perversities of the slum betrayed significant anxieties around the confinement of racialized populations. Fear of contamination is a central theme in both early colonial situations and the management of twentieth-century slums. As a repository for the unwanted elements of society, the degenerate zone posed a threat of contamination whose antidote was a respectable space in which to insulate one's family, and their race and class group.

Stallybrass and White have studied nineteenth-century 'reforming texts,' which survey the British lower and working classes, depicting conditions in great detail and advising as to their improvement. These texts – that century's equivalent of urban planning reports – when read critically, reveal how moral considerations of the time structure what are considered to be the most economic uses of space and the most efficient measures by which the slum might be 'cleaned up.' They also reveal a preoccupation with the study and surveillance of the lower classes and were directed toward the middle class, providing a way in which the bourgeois subject might 'see in' without crossing the borders of the ghetto. Fear of disease is central in these narratives as well, and regulation was set in place so that, for instance, prostitutes could be incarcerated if they were suffering from venereal disease. The slum is imagined, from the outside, as a large infectious body which can open and spill its contaminants, whether germs, persons, or conditions, into the space of the respectable masses. For example:

> the slum, the labouring poor, the prostitute, the sewer, were recreated for the bourgeois study and drawing room as much as for the urban council chamber. Indeed, the reformers were central in the construction of the urban geography of the bourgeois Imaginary. As the bourgeoisie produced new forms of regulation and prohibition governing their own bodies, they wrote ever more loquaciously of the body of the Other – of the city's 'scum.'[57]

Consistent with Foucault's formulation of biopower, governing subjects treated disease, like crime, as something which could be policed.[58]

Mariana Valverde has traced similar discourses in the Canadian context by examining middle-class concerns over cleaning up the slums of the early twentieth century.[59] This involved immigration policies that considered both the lower classes of England and non-white people as more likely carriers of sexually transmitted and other diseases. In particular, Valverde documents early efforts to prevent slum development in Canada like that in the United States and Europe. This concern involved morally inflected judgments about the health risks posed to the rest of society by the poor and racialized slum-dweller. Citing the frequent repetition of fears about 'disease, vice, and crime,' she demonstrates the necessary erasure of the subjectivity of slum residents and their representation by researchers and reformers. She notes a common emphasis on 'knowledge as control,' which gave way to vigilant observation and documentation of slum areas.

David Sibley is also attentive to the separation of respectable from degenerate spaces. He discusses the symbolic potency of race in shaping and maintaining the vigilance around such boundaries. In particular, he emphasizes the symbolic quality of whiteness as 'purity' that requires protection.

> whiteness is a symbol of purity, virtue and goodness and a colour which is easily polluted ... Thus, white may be connected with a heightened consciousness of the boundary between white and not-white, with an urge to clean, to expel dirt and resist pollution, whether whiteness is attributed to people or to material objects ... As a marker of the boundary between purified interior spaces – the home, the nation, and so on – and exterior threats posed by dirt, disorderly minorities or immigrants, white is still a potent symbol.[60]

Sibley notes that the interest in purity signals a specific dilemma for the dominant subject, and for conceptions of whiteness. As David Roediger has pointed out, 'whiteness' has essentially no meaning outside systems of domination of the racial Other. In other words, for governing subjects, racial identity becomes significant in reference to that which it *is not*.[61] So at the same time that dominant subjects are overtly concerned with instating and reinforcing the border between pure and contaminated peoples and places, there is a necessary fluidity to this border, which harkens back to Valverde and others' concern with knowledge of the Other. While allowing protection and isolation from the contaminants of the slum, the border must be porous enough that some measure of visibility is retained; it must allow the dominant subject the freedom of transgression and return.

While the subjects of analysis in my study, and various others, abide within the borders of racial apartheid, there does exist a 'contact zone' where privileged white people travel to the space of the Other, and where the privileged learn their dominance. As Mohanram reminds us, the black body is relegated to the slum, but dominant bodies are able to cross borders, to move, to explore at will. This phenomenon has been examined through dominant subjects' exploration and mapping of marginal spaces, but it also occurs through their engagement in the anomalous activities of such spaces.

The spaces of racial marginality are frequently viewed as zones where lawlessness prevails, and thus where deviant activity can take place without retribution. Anderson demonstrates how Vancouver's

Chinatown became an identifiable area for prostitution, drug abuse, and other illegal activity. Razack explores how, metaphorically and very physically at once, the anomalous zone of prostitution enables certain relations, organized through gender, race, and class. Through transgression into these spaces, the privileged (usually male) subject moves in and out of a dangerous and necessarily subjugated space. Transgression and return enable the sense that defilement remains behind, contained in the bodies and spaces of the Other, while the elite subject can escape contamination through return, and secure his dominance in doing so.[62]

Stallybrass and White identify a similar phenomenon in their depiction of 'the carnival,' a common concept in much nineteenth-century cultural and literary analysis. This refers broadly to large festivals and rituals in public space, of an exceptional character – contrary to everyday norms. In the carnival, the notion of exotic spaces and bodies offering spectacle and escape is central. As observed (and feared) from afar by the bourgeois subject, such occasions were seen as performances of gross excess and perverse, uninhibited behaviour of the masses. At the same time, fascination and desire propelled the *flaneur* toward the carnival as an act of transgression through the shedding of constrictive, respectable middle class norms for the limited permissible time.[63] A contemporary analogy might be Gay Pride parades, in which participants are free for a time to perform and exhibit aspects of their identities which are, from day-to-day, silenced and marginalized. This is consistent with Stallybrass and White's contention that 'carnival' may take on political meanings for those who initiate it, recoding the everyday relations of power and constituting an act of resistance, however fleeting, through visibility and disruption. At the same time, onlookers, like the *flaneur*, can gain and secure knowledge of their difference. They are free to consume the spectacle, to indulge in amusement, 'scandal,' or a taste for the exotic, while knowing that the status quo remains at home and, further, that these spaces entitle 'home' to be what it is.

Shifting Locations: Space over Time

At the beginning of the chapter I identified a few main contentions about space that are most salient for the purposes of my project. One was that the articulation of racial meanings and racism require space. Another was that subjects come to know themselves in their relationship to social spaces. Another was that the technologies by which spaces are managed along racial lines continue over time, even where they take on new and revised forms. As can be read in historical, postcolonial analyses, through to more recent theories of social space, whether overseas or 'at home,' race has long been the terrain on which the politics of spatial difference are written. Several theorists have studied how this occurs through quite dramatic shifts in political context over time. For instance, Lindsay Bremner traces the complex geographies of post-apartheid South Africa: Geographic boundaries which formerly served to contain white fears and racialized Others have been dismantled. Now, 'the stranger, the mob, the beast, that against which the entire edifice of apartheid had been erected, is within. Urban spaces have been rendered permeable, open to infiltration, intervention and contamination.'[64] Bremner relates this concern with newfound proximity (similar to Hesse's notion of the 'internal Other') to various other social contexts and to the results of immigration in Western cities, noting that:

> in almost all these contexts, the consequence has been the adoption of a new politics of closure, the identification of new figures on which to project and expect unbearable psychological material, and the emergence of new techniques of exclusion and withdrawal. These remake the cognitive map of social segregation in the city and construct new references through which everyday life and social relations can be lived.[65]

Eduardo Mendieta applies a Foucauldian reading to various racialized phenomena throughout U.S. history, including the plantation, Jim Crow laws, the urban ghetto, the prison, and death row, theorizing them as the foundational geopolitics of America. His historicized reading identifies the racialized ghetto as 'the racial geography that takes over the role of the plantation once the United States had abolished slavery.' In this, he suggests a methodology that accounts for the ongoing role of spatial containment and management through different eras, while examining the different forms these techniques take according to dominant demands. Uniting Foucault's formulations of power, knowledge, and bodily and social regulation, Mendieta writes: 'How we constitute ourselves as subjects has to do with the partitioning, distribution, linking, closing off, mapping, and the surveying of social space. The spaces that allow for certain truths to produce force effects and conversely, how certain powers produced certain truths, are spaces that come to bear upon the individual as a body.'[66]

Mendieta consistently names the body as the essential target of regulatory power; rarely is this effect more apparent than in the literal removal of housing, and of bodies from spaces. In the mid-twentieth century, as North American cities became increasingly shamed by the stain of poverty on their landscapes, slum removal replaced slum management as a central formula by which to manage the poor and racialized. As Kay Anderson notes, Vancouver's Chinatown came to be depicted as a tumour, threatening to spread were it not excised, and indicating that 'Chinatown's diagnosis as a "slum" was to be justified and realized through the surgery itself.'[67]

Such a surgical analogy, broadly applied, describes the displacement of various racialized communities, in many contexts. Beginning in 1963, very close to the time of Africville's 'relocation,' the Canadian government began to move the Ojibwa people of the Grassy Narrows reserve in Northern Ontario to a new reserve several miles from their original home. Justified through the promise of progress (better schools, services, and housing), the move proved devastating to their way of life.[68] This move was part of a larger body of relocation plans that the government commonly enacted in Native communities in the 1960s.

In North American cities, displacement meant that residents were evicted from the slums and moved to public housing projects built specifically for this purpose. Municipalities constructed low-rent, high density housing projects in central areas of cities, but surrounded them with isolating features such as rail lines, vacant lots, or public parks. This, along with their highly visible structure, contained residents in zones that facilitated their observation by outsiders. With slum residents piled neatly on top of one another, their former territories could be converted to respectable commercial or residential space and sold or rented at higher prices.

Africville's destruction must be understood at this juncture, where the history of slum establishment and management meets that of urban 'clean up' and the reconfinement of racialized communities in the projects. Various theorists have documented the shifting strategies of compression and containment that served to effectively maintain segregation through the twentieth century, particularly in response to the increased migration of southern U.S. blacks to northern cities.[69] For example, Arnold Hirsch has analysed the growth of post–Second World War black ghetto areas in Chicago with careful attention to the city's history of violent racial struggle. He argues that the mid-century reconfiguration of geographic boundaries within the city – essentially a new mode of segregation – was spurred by white panic over the increased migration of southern blacks to the northern city, combined with particular political and economic interests. A combination of economic-driven public policy and physical violence characterized the creation of the era's urban ghetto.[70]

Dominant society knows the ghetto or 'the projects' as the contemporary configuration of the slum – a site of delinquency, social turmoil, and contagion. As Goldberg writes, 'the projects present a generic image without identity: the place of crime; of social disorder, dirt and disease; of teenage pregnancy, prostitution, pimps, and drug dependency; the workless and shiftless, disciplined internally if at all only by social welfare workers.'[71] Thus, the alleged progress of slum clearance and urban renewal was not realized as the just and desegregating phenomenon it professed to be. Rather, cities moved to a new phase of spatial ordering – but it is one in which 'social problems' are simply relocated. Rather than resulting in a systemic analysis of poverty and racism, the practice of slum removal perpetuates a common public view that the blight, the slum, moves with the bodies of the poor and racialized, remaining entrenched within them. Governments have simply updated modes of enclosure and observation, underscoring the chasms in the relations they make possible.

Allan Pred studies the development of urban ghettos in Sweden as the country's immigrant population has increased. He notes how depictions of the slum or project in contemporary discourse contribute to knowledge about the racial Other in both real and 'imagined' ways, through, 'negative and often contradictory significations repeatedly evoked by discourse and representation, the frequent metaphoric and metonymic usage of these place names, the telling and retelling of symbol-laden stories about these concrete spaces, [which] contributes to the perpetuation and legitimation of discrimination toward migrant and refugee residents.'[72]

Pred's analysis attends to both concrete place and the meanings it evokes. While discourses about race may seem to merely accompany spatial arrangements, they accomplish a great deal more than this. They structure how spatial arrangements play out, making them appear natural. Spaces in turn influence discourse, seeming to offer concrete evidence, through the physical environment, that the discourse is correct. This is a cycle with metaphoric aspects, and the space/subjectivity dialectic is a useful discursive model, but it is simultaneously crucial to see how it organizes material life. For those on the less privileged end of the spectrum, this can mean water contamination, unemployment, lower access to healthcare; it means that the police don't come when called, or that children receive inadequate education. As a community 'becomes' a slum, then, those in society's dominant spaces are offered evidence, in its defilement, that their perceptions of its space and its residents are true to form: it *is* decrepit; there *is* more crime; education levels are lower, unemployment higher. The timeless problem of 'what to do about it' also becomes a vicious cycle, in that what is done, what has been done, and what will again be done are strands of the intricate web of a history built of violence, displacement, and racism.

History Takes Place

Nova Scotia is a winding peninsular section of the Atlantic coast with a population of less than one million. It is damp, with a short summer, almost entirely Christian (Protestant) and it just recently became legal for its stores to be open on Sunday. Incomes are below the national average; unemployment is high. It is roughly and strikingly beautiful, with a stony, jagged coastline that contains rich, green farmland. It has become a popular vacation spot and summer residence for wealthy Americans and other Canadians. It has a long-established black community – the oldest in Canada. It has particular, regional English and French expressions and accents, a particular humour and a pride in its Celtic origins and music. About 17,000 Mi'kmaq live in the province, most on its twenty-three reserves.[73]

The world port of Halifax sits on the coast where Europeans first landed in Canada. It is steeped in British naval history, yet it has been the first point of entry for vastly diverse groups of people, whether they remained there or not. Many visitors describe it as welcoming and warm. Others, often people of colour, describe difficulties in renting apartments, and are surprised by the continued, visible segregation.

I live in Toronto, where nearly every Monday morning I read in the local paper how many young black men were shot over the weekend – and the places where it happens are always the same. In Vancouver, I lived near the lower east side and had the new experience, daily, of encountering displaced, homeless urban Aboriginal people asking for food or money. While living in Montreal, I often witnessed a vehement, angry fear of immigrants, especially those of colour, who would dilute and pollute a francophone nation. I notice now in Halifax how little non-white skin I see. I have forgotten to notice in Toronto that typically at least half of the people on the bus are of colour, but when taking a bus in Halifax, I note their absence.

The point of this analysis is never to suggest that Nova Scotia is 'more racist' or 'less racist' than anywhere else; rather, its racism is particular to its own history and its own geography (as is the case everywhere). Throughout Africville's story, there are shadows of a particular whiteness in operation; it is specific to its time and place, no more or less potent than other examples of racialized histories and societies. There are, of course, commonalities in racisms too, especially in their underlying intents and effects. There is a way in which racisms allow dominant subjects a common articulation of sameness and difference. A man from a rural area recently told me that 'when you go to Toronto now, you feel like a stranger.' I didn't understand at first; but he explained: he was referring to the supposed hordes of immigrants, bursting the floodgates, threatening 'our' sense of belonging. A woman I encountered in downtown Toronto made similar comments about Vancouver, referring to the increasing number of mosques and Hindu temples marking its landscape: 'It doesn't feel Canadian anymore.' White people talk to each other this way; there is an implicit assumption of common knowledge, of agreement as to who is a legitimate citizen and who a stranger – an axiom that 'we' know what it means to be rightful owners and occupants of a place under seige by Others. In particular, dominant subjects know what looks, feels, and *is* Canadian. This is part of the nationalist and racialist language of whiteness that can seem as natural as the air we breathe.[74]

How do we know difference, then, when a black community has existed in a Canadian place for 250 years? When its ancestors arrived as Loyalists along with whites, or as refugees from American slavery? How, when eighty black homes have sat clustered on the banks of the harbour for over one hundred years with their church, their school, their stores, do we know that they don't belong? When a person could receive a letter from anywhere addressed, simply, to 'Africville, Nova Scotia,' how is it that Africville was marked as Other, as Outside? Lines must be starkly drawn for such knowledge to have meaning. They must be redrawn as often as necessary so that difference always makes sense.

Such lines were drawn around Africville from the beginning; it was denied, neglected, placed out of society and beyond law, and allowed to deteriorate until it *was* a slum, and the residents slum-dwellers. Still, white people entered Africville. They entered for fun and passed out on doorsteps; they entered to leave their garbage behind. They entered to study and observe, to report, to coerce, and to rescue. And when it finally became too visibly defiled, they entered to remove people and to flatten homes, to level and transform the land, and to encrypt it with new meaning. They enter now to look at the ocean, or to attempt to make sense of an enduring absence. This geography is one of deliberate transformation, not accident. In this landscape, space, subject, and power are braided. This is where Africville lived, and this is how it was razed.

3 Knowing Africville: Telling Stories of Blackness

> Whoever does the initial report ... is really making the decision. That was really the atmosphere in which it was done.
>
> Halifax Alderman, interviewed about the Africville decision[1]

What do we accomplish through study, through observation, through interviewing, through participating? What do we learn by watching, talking, joining, policing, entering and leaving a place? How do we remember the nature of a place and its people? How is this knowledge passed on, employed to inform others? How does it come to constitute truth and reality?

White ideologies about black community and the consistency with which they appear offer a framework that starkly illuminates the racialization of Africville. During the 1950s and 1960s, white city officials and professionals observed, analysed, policed, and wrestled with the existence of the black community in their midst. Politicians, urban planners, police, social workers, academics, and journalists alike perceived and portrayed black identity as, variably, a threat, a pathological problem, and an object of pity or disdain. In this light, they studied and narrated Africville, too, as a place outside society, fit only for the wastes and production processes of the mainstream, and dispensable when it grew too visibly polluted. They constituted the black community as distinctly Other, as infantile, directionless, and unable to rationally participate in the planning of its future. They characterized black space as existing outside civilized society, and as ultimately obsolete. The data to be explored in this chapter delineate the central story of race and Otherness produced in white Nova Scotia in the era preceding, accompanying, and following the destruction of Africville. Many disciplines and many discourses contributed to this project.

The great challenge is to illustrate these key discourses through the linear ordering of ideas demanded by language. To say that they are interdependant, that they constitute one another, seems woefully inadequate. However, I proceed with the image in mind of a circular thread, with no end and no beginning, that loops back upon itself time and time again in different directions, forming a giant knot. To loosen any section of the knot would affect the whole, changing the shape and position of all its other segments. For the black community to be understood as outside the bounds of normative society, it is necessary to see the culture of residents as deviant, criminal; in order to make sense of this deviance, it is necessary to understand blackness as savage, uncivilized. To uphold notions of incivility, one must call up, and denigrate, black culture, values, ways of life; these in turn can be linked to the filth, the slums where people live. Their continued existence in such spaces must be explained, and this is accomplished through the attribution of irrationality, inferior intelligence, and dependence. As they are unable, or unwilling, to see their own way out of their situations, they must be policed, regulated, or rescued. If they cannot be rescued and managed, it is further evidence of their inherent deviance, their natural 'apartness' on the margins. And so on. The discourses, then, are interwoven strands of an effective 'common sense' logic.

The sources explored here (newspapers, city officials, government reports) represent the key sites of the racial knowledge that made Africville's destruction possible. The analysis of these sources calls on Foucault's connection between power and knowledge – they were the ones that garnered the power to dominate, to inform public discourse. They are not simply interesting for their own sake, but for what they made it possible to *do*. Africville's destruction is situated within larger discourses of urban development during the mid-century; Africville is described as antithetical to this development, as a place outside normal, dominant society. In order for this displacement from society to make sense, I argue, whites accessed a body of knowledge about blacks that was readily available through academic and popular discourses of cultural pathology. Further, they employed notions of such pathology to justify intensive regulation and the need for discipline of black communities. This discipline extended, in the reports I explore, from consideration of individual family problems to the need for broad-based community policing. White writers consistently inscribe black bodies as irrational, which serves to justify their control and direction by white authorities.

A journalist from the *New York Times* who visited Halifax in 1964 best encapsulated the climate of racism and poverty around the time of Africville's destruction. He stated that blacks 'knew the rules' as to where they could and could not go. Public space remained deeply segregated, and the same author observed that black residents of Halifax were denied service in some restaurants, barbershops, and hotels.[2] A *Maclean's* article, too, documented the difficulties for Halifax blacks of renting apartments, and noted, following research, that some restaurants would not serve the black men who entered.[3] Societal values of segregation invaded the private sphere as well. In a news article from 1966, various white ministers from around the province were interviewed as to the church's views on interracial marriage. While a few expressed a polite tolerance, most stated reservations, and a few were blatantly opposed, citing the Bible as a moral guide that denounces the mixing of the races.[4]

Economic conditions, too, remained dismal. Donald Clairmont and Dennis Magill noted in 1970 that 90 per cent of the Halifax black population lived below the poverty level with incomes under $3000 per year (while 25 per cent of whites fell into this category).[5] A report from a 1969 conference at St Francis Xavier University confirmed that most of the province's 15,000 black residents lived below the poverty level, in small communities outside the major towns and cities, and received few or drastically inferior services. One speaker particularly addressed the lack of consultation with communities affected by planning. Urban planners of the time noted extremely poor housing conditions among blacks, half of whom lacked bathing facilities and three quarters hot water.[6]

A white human rights lawyer who visited Halifax in 1962 observed what he called a particularly Canadian flavour of racism during this period, embodied in 'the gentleman bigot,' who practises discrimination in a seemingly 'courteous and disarming manner.'[7] He echoed the sentiment that blacks knew the rules as to where they could go, and were constantly vigilant about the possibility of encountering racism in white spaces.

Progress

Halifax's regeneration plans were part of the larger pattern of urban clean up throughout North America in the 1950s and 1960s. Planners and government officials, under such plans, aimed to remove decrepit, rundown areas and to move their residents to public housing projects.[8] While they assured improvements in housing, services, access to education, and job opportunities – which were important to their potential recipients – these promises frequently dissolved into the simple removal of rundown areas for the sake of ridding the city of embarrassment and creating economic opportunity for business and industry. Those uprooted and cleared out were usually low-income families; many were racial minorities. These families typically lost their homes and were placed in rental units in public housing. During the 1950s and 1960s, the city of Halifax built four major housing projects and completed several urban planning and housing development studies.

Urban renewal, when closely examined, continued a colonial-style project of spatial management and containment in profound ways. Since it operated under the rubric of liberal ideas about integration, this aspect has often been overlooked. The concerns of urban reformers and social engineers consistently reflect racial marking, which is often coded in discourses about 'the poor.' These ideas, incorporated in government policy, backed an assumed need to better control deviant populations, whose values and behaviours would tarnish white urban space.

David Goldberg's work on slum administration posits that specific spatial planning technologies merely shift over time, but that these shifts do not significantly effect the containment of racialized populations. He defines a shift in urban planning motives in the West after the Second World War away from concerns with city beautification toward an emphasis on social efficiency, until roughly 1960. Around this time, concerns with efficiency were developed into a more complex rational system of development and resource management. Goldberg acknowledges that planning ideology did not develop simply in response to a desire to control marginalized social groups. However, he demonstrates the effects of this shift on the racially marked, as well as how issues of racial difference considerably influenced the growth and utilization of such planning initiatives.[9]

In 1956, Halifax city council, the provincial government of Nova Scotia, and the Central Mortgage and Housing Corporation commissioned Professor Gordon Stephenson, of the Town and Regional

Planning Department of the University of Toronto, to study housing conditions in the city of Halifax. His mandate was to suggest which areas required redevelopment, how families occupying these areas should be rehoused, and how the cleared areas would best be used.[10] Formerly, federal funding for redevelopment could only be obtained where land would be used for low-cost housing. Stephenson's study was carried out shortly after federal legislation had been changed; under the new policy, land could be funded and redeveloped for its 'highest and best use,' the determination of which was left to municipal authorities. Federal policy on national defence had been expanded, creating a demand for dockyard and harbour-front space, as well as for improved railway facilities to and from these sites.[11] Further, while the city was experiencing an enduring economic high point following the Second World War, the recent expansion of the Great Lakes–St Lawrence Seaway posed an economic threat to the port. The city feared its inability to compete in a wave of increased efficiency and industrial development that would result from greater access to inland ports along the St Lawrence River.[12]

Economic conditions and rapid growth also demanded the reconsideration of housing patterns.[13] The municipality was eager to move forward with plans to centralize businesses, justify industrial expansion, and remove neighbourhoods deemed undesirable. In this context, Stephenson's report, *A Redevelopment Study of Halifax, Nova Scotia*, conveys many concerns over the management of poor and minority families, and a sense of where these groups were seen to fit in the modern scheme of development. About Africville, he wrote:

> There is a little frequented part of the City, overlooking Bedford Basin, which presents an unusual problem for any community to face. In what may be described as an encampment, or shack town, there live some seventy negro families ...
>
> The citizens of Africville live a life apart. On a sunny day, the small children swim in what amounts to their private lagoon. In winter, life is far from idyllic. In terms of the physical condition of buildings and sanitation, the story is deplorable. Shallow wells and cesspools, in close proximity, are scattered about the slopes between the shacks.
>
> There are only two things to be said. The families will have to be rehoused in the near future. The land which they now occupy will be required for the future development of the City. A solution which is satisfactory, socially as well as economically, will be difficult to achieve.

Africville stands as an indictment of society and not of its inhabitants. They are old Canadians who have never had the opportunities enjoyed by their more fortunate fellows.[14]

This excerpt from the Stephenson report has become one of the most widely quoted depictions of both the nature of Africville and the alleged inevitability of its destruction. The passage summarizes his analysis and conclusion about Africville's future. It comprises the official story about the community put forth in the white public domain and accepted among some blacks as well. The text invokes themes that became common in dominant public discourse – for example, Africville as slum, Africville as outside the bounds of society, and the axiom that Africville's space required clearing and redevelopment.

The depiction of Africville as a problem 'difficult for any community to face,' suggests what is considered to be – *and not to be* – 'the community.' Its 'life apart' begs the question, 'apart from *what?*' The place is described as 'little frequented' while it is home to 400 people. Similar sentiments were expressed by another visiting researcher, who stated, 'You might just as well assume no one was living there,'[15] and by a journalist from *Maclean's* magazine, who described a nearby black community as a place where 'no one' went. Imposing on land needed for 'development of the city,' and threatening the city's borders (even though it was there first), Africville becomes *not* part of the city; it is antithetical to development.[16] This and other reports explicitly assume that the community is already slated for removal,[17] even though the decision had not been declared official; for instance, a newspaper article describes the community as 'doomed.'[18]

In the text of another study, the *Halifax Region Housing Survey*, author H.S. Coblentz stresses that Halifax can grow no further without careful urban planning. He recommends the establishment of a governing body that would unify housing guidelines to 'harmonize the future competing demands for land.'[19] This survey displays a clear awareness that large numbers of black people have been and will continue to be displaced over the next few years. Plans to move Africville are specifically mentioned in this regard.[20] Coblentz notes that housing conditions had greatly improved over the past decade in the city as a whole, while remaining drastically substandard for most low-income and black families. He is not unsympathetic to the situation of these populations, and criticizes the haphazard, case-by-case manner in which housing has been structured up to this point. He notes that minority populations will face special difficulties if displaced from their homes. However, he gives no detail of what these difficulties are, and cites them as being of particular concern because of the cost they might pose to the city itself, and due to the effect they may have on other neighbourhoods where residents might end up.[21]

Coblentz states concern that 'minority' interests can delay progress on 'controversial issues.' He also notes that regulations are required to keep 'undesirable' people out of neighbourhoods. In general, the survey supports relocation and public housing. It is primarily concerned with careful documentation, or 'human bookkeeping,' to track lower income and racial minority groups as to what occurs when they move from one area to another – for instance, to see that another slum area does not develop. Coblentz notes that Halifax particularly needs these statistics 'since the region has the highest percentage of negroes in Canada.'[22]

Similar to planning reports, the media often depicts Africville as a *place apart*.[23] One article notes the 'growing acres of wasteland' that someday may be used by the city.[24] News reports describe a growing urban economy in which Africville is already left behind, and residents are seen as ignorant of its inevitable future. For example, an article states: 'Some of the conditions which influence the desire of the families to remain in the area will disappear as more attention is focused on the area.'[25] News articles often betray fear of the spread of blight to the rest of the city. Africville is portrayed much like the purported 'tumour' of Vancouver's Chinatown, and the press frequently urges faster action on its excision, as is evident from headlines such as 'Procrastination on Africville Should Be Ended' and 'Africville: Time for Action Is Now.'[26]

Cultures of Poverty

In the documents examined here, black communities are displaced from notions of progress and development in modern Halifax society. I am concerned with tracing the discourses that were employed to displace these communities, and with how these discourses came to be commonly accepted sociological terms of the time. Larry Bennett and Adolph Reed have examined the legacy of sociological theories surrounding urban poverty that developed throughout the twentieth century. They find both materially and in academic theory, class and race are interwoven to identify the nature of 'social pathology' in slum and ghetto areas.[27]

Academic and popular literature in the latter half of the twentieth century strongly articulated formulations of pathology, as cultural explanations tended to supplant biological theories of racial difference. Philomena Essed examines this shift, positing that while the legacy of biological theory remains, blacks have more recently been targeted by newer discourses. She writes:

> Cultural arguments are used more and more to blame Blacks themselves for the situation of poverty and their slow rise in the system compared with White immigrants and Asians ... Underlying this discourse is the implication that Euro-American cultural standards are uncritically accepted as the norm and positive standard. The traditional idea of genetic inferiority is still important in the fabric of racism, but the discourse of Black inferiority is increasingly formulated as cultural deficiency, social inadequacy, and technological underdevelopment.[28]

Theories of cultural deficiency were gaining credibility in governmental and planning discourses by the time of Africville's destruction. Goldberg has posited that the concentration of poor and racialized groups in defined urban spaces serves to perpetuate notions of their pathology.

> The concentration effect exacerbates the products of a racially exclusionary poverty by concentrating them in a containable space easily avoidable by those not so confined. Conservative commentators largely emphasize the pathological character of the racialized poor as the overriding causal consideration in extending their poverty. So the concentration effect is not just spatial; it is also ideological.[29]

The thinking Goldberg describes is based in 'culture-of-poverty' theories, whose origins can be traced to the early twentieth century in the Chicago School,[30] particularly in the work of Oscar Lewis.[31] Bennett and Reed note that this approach fails to consider the influence of public policy and political action in shaping the supposedly 'natural environment' in which residents live. Instead, concentration is focused on the more easily discernible physical surroundings and individual and family circumstances. They trace this theoretical bent to the formation of narratives about the 'deserving' and the 'undeserving' poor. At this junction some populations become more explicitly racialized, creating, for example, a narrative of the black ghetto as the home of uncontrolled, degenerate, and therefore undeserving people. The latter are seen to bring poor conditions with them wherever they move,[32] meaning that any space they inhabit will be potentially at risk. Control of space is a primary mode of policing the borders between respectability and degeneracy.

Notions of an innate culture of poverty, consummated in the 1960s, have been influential well beyond sociological academic circles, making their way throughout public debate and into policy decisions. The Moynihan report on the black family,[33] for instance, took up the cultural argument in proclaiming social pathology as the cause of black poverty, launching approaches to policy and research that emphasized individual defective behaviour and values among the poor black population. Social reform became largely a matter of rehabilitating the individuals and areas in question, rather than examining or challenging the systemic causes.

Bennett and Reed also analyse how narratives of social pathology enabled an appearance of empathy and non-racist sentiment. They write, 'Lewis's culture-of-poverty formulation gave those who were uncomfortable with frankly racist stereotypes a way to embrace a fundamentally racialized theory of the defective poor while avoiding the stigma of racism. Culture became a proxy for race.'[34] In this vein, whites could support research initiatives in favour of displacing poor and racialized groups while espousing concern for their conditions. The well meaning social theorist could indulge an interest in the plight of the black community, tip her hat to anti-racism, yet never leave the causal parameters of the community's own borders and culture.

A shift from biological to cultural rationalizations for racial inferiority does not erase the narrative of inferiority itself. Further, conditions in economically deprived areas still become entangled with the identities of residents and cognitively attached, in the white imagination, to the body of the racial Other. It is this process that the term 'racialization' encapsulates. In this context, it foregrounds how blacks and the areas they inhabit are marginalized and marked as Other. It is not only discourses of race and culture that infuse this marking; norms of sexuality and gender roles figure centrally in defining the behaviour and values under question in analyses of black culture.

'Embourgeoisement,' a term used by Clairmont and Magill in the *Africville Relocation Report*, refers to the enforcement of middle-class material and moral standards in family and living arrangements, which were imposed on communities like Africville. For instance, values such as privacy and personal space are often presented as universal standards for a normal healthy lifestyle. The fact that poor communities may benefit from the closer sharing of resources and skills, which is not necessary in more privileged groups, is absent from consideration. It has often been noted that Africville's sense of community came in part from extended family networks that developed over the years through sharing of living space, handing down of properties, and the cooperation required to survive with few financial resources. Older people tended to be cared for at home, and children tended to find food and shelter in the houses of various friends, which would be reciprocated in their own. In urban planning models, extended families living in shared spaces are considered evidence of a community's degeneracy. For instance, a social work student involved in a commissioned study of Halifax blacks expresses great consternation over families who were living in various non-nuclear arrangements, and describes this disorder as 'family breakdown.'[35]

In the 1950s and 1960s, and generally still, heterosexual marriage and the patriarchal nuclear family form the ideal type of household. Racialized notions of proper gender roles contributed to a view of the black family as unviable. Susan Precious, writing about women in Africville, describes how black women have historically been viewed, through slavery and beyond, as fit for any required labour, in contrast to white women, whose assumed virtue and delicacy required protection.[36] The figure of the 'lady' has historically depended on the labour of lower-class and black women whose roles and personas reflect the antithesis of the lady's subjectivity. At the same time, black women's roles as wage earners and household heads have been used to pathologize the black family, as it cannot possibly conform to dominant ideals.[37] White bourgeois family norms and ideals, as will be seen, permeate the urban planning, academic, and media discourses herein.

So what does the mapping of cultural pathology look like 'on the ground'? An illustration can be seen in a book entitled *Forgotten Canadians*, which documents a study of Nova Scotian blacks over the last years of the 1960s. The author, Frances Henry, describes her study as an investigation of the values of the black community, the purpose of which is to determine if there is a distinct black subculture, different from mainstream white culture. She draws explicitly on a 'culture of poverty' framework and engages discourse about the values of poor and racial minority groups. She also employs 'value stretch' theory, which suggests that lower-class groups adopt the values of the middle class but, since these are unattainable, adjust their tolerance level to accept circumstances and behaviours that may be incompatible with dominant value systems.[38]

After living in several different communities for months at a time, and having graduate students interview the residents, Henry concludes that Nova Scotian black culture has no distinct content, having simply grown from the values and beliefs of white society. 'Deviance' from white, middle-class values, however, is practised and accepted. She attributes this to the necessity of adaptation in order to reduce frustration, while noting that the inability to achieve dominant norms stems from structural patterns of racism. She takes the U.S. black communities as sites of comparison and attributes an alleged lack of cohesiveness in Nova Scotia to the absence of historical plantation slave culture, which forced American blacks to unite and develop separate subcultural traditions.

The study makes various assertions that are not viewed in comparison with any other groups, black or white. For instance, the author writes that blacks are highly critical of anyone among them who strives for upward mobility and engage in putdowns, which she calls 'leveling.' This behaviour is described as a way to jealously discourage anyone from 'moving up' socially and economically.[39] She also writes that blacks engage in a great deal of gossip, that young men often brag about their sexual exploits and that the people talk about sex frequently, that the population is composed of heavy drinkers and that many people believe in witchcraft.[40] Since the study has identified a central goal as the dissipation of myths and the accurate reporting of objective data, and since some stereotypes *are* actually thwarted, these assertions are lent an air of credibility.

Henry employs highly arbitrary and simplistic tools of measurement, such as a 'race relations scale' and a series of 'values pictures.' For instance, interviewees are shown a picture of a younger and an older man who appear to be having an argument. When the majority suggest that this is a father/son argument, Henry concludes that this is evidence of a large amount of father/son conflict in the community. When asked to choose a preferred picture from two, one with a family in which two men are arguing, and one with a family calmly watching television together, interviewees chose the second. This was seen as evidence that they preferred a 'happy, contented and quiet home.'[41]

Other modes of measuring values are similarly crude – for instance, the researchers ask residents if they consider themselves to be poor, if

others consider them poor, and whether they consider themselves to
be 'as good as whites.' (They are said to have responded to such questions with 'hostility.') When the vast majority claim, on surveys, to
have little problem with whites, Henry contends that blacks fail to see
the racism around them and simply accept their inferior positions as a
natural part of life.[42]

Many experts of the time describe the black community's inevitable
demise through a moral discourse that transparently draws on concerns about the community's need for discipline and regulation. The
Stephenson report is deeply concerned, for instance, with the discipline of children. Those living in poor conditions are assumed to
receive little guidance, a fact attributed to '"bad parents" and "bad"
children, with a general background of poor living and broken homes.'
The author goes on to note that in wealthier neighbourhoods it is usually sufficient just to 'warn parents' of a disciplinary problem, which
they are then capable of resolving on their own.[43] Poor children are
said to 'roam the streets' and get into more trouble; conditions in
which they live, and unsuitable home environments, are seen as
responsible for this behaviour. Stephenson discusses the consequences
of deficient child rearing as costly to the state, which must deal with
removing them from their homes and supporting them through social
welfare agencies. Another report, supported by the same academic
institute, echoes many of these concerns, and cites 'unmarried mothers
who keep their babies and work only sporadically' as an example of
the socio-economic problems 'associated at least partly with race.'
Even where the report focuses on larger scale employment problems
and the societal peer pressure for children to drop out of school, it references the lack of 'normal family patterns' as part of the issue.[44]

Such views about the poor and their parenting, however, did not
begin in the development studies of the mid-century. J.J. Kelso has
documented a history of the management of delinquent children in
Canada and the establishment of reform schools and agencies to conduct the socializing work that parents of the lower classes were seen
to neglect.[45] Discourses about the degeneracy of poor and racialized
families were part of a larger network of ideas linking crime to poverty. Stephenson speculates that 'overcrowding and shockingly bad
sanitary conditions must produce strife.' He links disturbances and
assaults cognitively to shared conditions of filth, and puts forth a
strict definition of proper family life, centred around 'a man, his wife
and their children' who could not possibly live in 'harmony' while

poor. He concludes that 'the clearance of the worst housing should reduce the work and the costs of the police force'.[46]

While these assertions are not always explicitly connected to race, they do constitute common narratives of the racial slum, and the report makes clear a concern with minority populations in particular.[47] In keeping with the character of racism at the time,[48] social problems are not usually blamed overtly on the class or race origins of the residents, but rather, on the conditions in which they live. Using only one reference, to a professor whose work itself is not identified, Stephenson writes that 'Juvenile delinquency is a sign of mental ill health.' He argues that psychologists and social workers consistently find the moral and emotional character of a child's home, much more than socio-economic circumstances, to be central in creating delinquent behaviour.[49] This supports a psychological, individualized model of crime and delinquency that is removed from its social cause and context.

Policing the Slum

The phenomenon of racialized crime is not without its own history. Documenting the treatment of criminality in Halifax in the early twentieth century, Michael Boudreau presents the criminalization of racial minority groups as a factor that further entrenched their marginality. Their presence provided the police with a ready pool of scapegoats in an era of social and economic unrest, when concern for maintaining social order reached prodigious heights.[50]

While the working class white man was constructed as a prime suspect, the small black and Chinese populations of the city were recipients of a disproportionate amount of policing, suspicion, and violence from white citizens, as well as the Royal Canadian Mounted Police (RCMP). Boudreau demonstrates the long history and contemporary legacy of this climate of fear and violence through documentation of various racist acts. He cites the attempted lynching of a black man rumoured to have attacked a white child in 1918, as well as other such threats or attempts, including a cross-burning by the Ku Klux Klan outside a Halifax church in 1932.[51] He describes various racial riots in which white citizens attacked Chinese laundries or restaurants, believing them to be fronts for illicit gambling, drug smuggling, and prostitution of white girls. Sheridan Hay also notes an incident from 1946 in which the police shot an Africville man in the back as he ran away after being pulled over.[52] The report of this violence in the local paper appeared under the heading of, simply, 'Africville,' even though neither the driving nor the shooting took place there.

In the early twentieth century, the white community was profoundly fearful of a possible influx of white slavery, even though no significant evidence of such a threat has ever been found. Whites targeted both Chinese and black men,[53] commonly singling out blacks as the culprits of prostitution, and Chinese businesses as sites of gambling operations, while overlooking white gambling in various downtown hotels.

Boudreau also analyses a conflation of ethnic and criminalized populations, whereby minority groups are relegated to the status – and the spaces – of drunks, gamblers, and prostitutes.[54] Spatially distinct from respectable society, these groups constituted what Donald Clairmont has described as 'deviance service centres' – spaces apart from the usual function of morality and law, which could be visited for the consumption of illicit goods or activities.[55] Making links with Kay Anderson's work on Vancouver's Chinatown, Boudreau speaks of a small-scale Chinatown in Halifax, which was seen from outside to present similar threats to white society through the corruption of its young women and the promotion of drugs and gambling.[56] He speaks similarly of Africville's reputation as a place beyond the law where whites travelled to gamble or drink. This allowed clear lines to be drawn between the respectable and the criminal; while whites could participate freely in deviant activity, the criminal character could remain attached to the space and bodies of the slum.

In this light, it is not surprising that an intensive program of surveillance of the black population of Nova Scotia was carried out around the time of Africville's destruction. In the mid 1990s, the Canadian Press obtained a report documenting undercover surveillance that had been carried out by the RCMP during the 1960s and 1970s.[57] Charles Saunders, a prominent local historian, writes that police were alarmed over a supposed influx by the American Black Panther organization. Although a few people in Halifax had contact with a few of the Black Panthers, who had come on one occasion to observe and discuss black activism in Halifax, there is little evidence that the black community in general held links to this organization. Both Saunders and activist Rocky Jones have noted that the movement never gained significant weight in Canada and the population of Halifax was too small to create enough interest or support for the group's radical views.[58]

Even if the RCMP were obligated to investigate, their surveillance extended well beyond the dictates of an isolated visit by activists. It lasted for many years, and the data they collected had as much to do with the character of black communities and families as with any rebellious activity they might plan. Police, through a network of agents and informants, went undercover into black nightclubs, attended community meetings, and kept a close eye on university campuses, airports, and the Canadian border. They also closely watched other communities, well outside Halifax and apart from the scene of alleged political unrest. A July 1968 RCMP file about the black community in Guysborough County echoes common discourses about black families and culture: 'In this particular group, the women work steadily to support the family, which usually numbers quite a few small children, while the men work long enough to make money for another liquor binge. The children of these families are left to their own resources, becoming wild, unruly and unclean.'[59] It later continues, 'The Negro birthrate is extremely high and the number of individuals striving for education beyond Grade 8 is very low. It is not for the lack of education facilities or poor standards.'

Other files show that the police have been tracking the precise activities of one person 'since quitting school,' and of two 'American negroes' who visit their families in the Preston area each year. Reports document the surveillance of youths in small groups as well as individuals thought to have any radical political sentiments. For example, an August 1969 report states: 'There are a few colored youths in this area who like to think of themselves as Black Panthers. This group, at the most 10 people, occasionally roll a drunk, etc. I suppose they feel it is more flattering to be referred to as Panthers than as thieves.' The police also speculate about the character of people believed to be potential activists, stating that one is 'a heavy drinker with a problem' and concluding about another: 'Aside from (name deleted), (name deleted) seems to be the only enthused new Panther with a marked degree of intelligence. Although the Black Panther movement is gaining ground, their disciples consist mainly of the illiterate, semi-illiterate and hoodlums.'[60]

The consequences of this surveillance are not fully known, but some Halifax residents experienced extremely invasive tracking of their daily activities. Rocky and Joan Jones, both politically active in Halifax, were closely monitored for eleven years, during which time their phone was tapped, they were followed home, and their mail was intercepted. They reported frequently seeing officers on stake-outs in front of their house. During this period, their store was ransacked and their home set on fire twice.[61]

In 1994, after the offending files were released, the RCMP apologized, under much pressure, and only through the media, to the black community. The Nova Scotia legislature publicly denounced the former surveillance practices. However, it remains clear that in the 1960s and 1970s, black lives and spaces were besieged by an intensive and unrelenting white gaze.

Crossing the Tracks

Many observations by whites about Africville, and Nova Scotian black communities generally, have a particular common current that is somewhat difficult to pin down empirically. I can best describe it as a mixture of fascination and revulsion that is nevertheless irresistible to its authors. There is something desirous, almost obsessive, about the gaze they apply to racialized spaces and bodies and the detail with which they describe them. I was initially taken by this breadth of description for what it could tell me analytically. As I became more aware of it, I cut down some of the more extensive quotations because I feared further entrenching this white gaze by replicating it.

Some articles betray a palpable excitement, a pleasure, that comes from transgressing social mores and spatial boundaries. Shortly before the period of Africville's destruction, coinciding with the early planning stages, a popular Canadian national news magazine, *Maclean's*, published an article about a Nova Scotia black community.[62] The author, Edna Staebler, spent a week studying a place she calls New Road settlement (a pseudonym), which is just outside the Halifax-Dartmouth area. Staebler foregrounds rumours she has heard about the community, which include fear-inducing tales of violence, fights among women, cults begun by superstitious residents, and police and city workers' fears of going in. Described as 'the most depressed area in Canada,'[63] New Road's attraction for Staebler grows with each new rumour she hears. Soon she can 'hardly wait to get out there, no matter how dangerous or dirty it might be.' Staebler describes the journey into a strange and exotic place 'almost as obscure and sinister as a village in an African jungle.' She describes 'jungle paths littered with excrement.' She reports in close detail the characteristics of every body she encounters. First is a 'very dark man,' soon followed by a 'dark brown young woman' and some 'ebony black boys.' Her subjects range in colour 'from jet black to light brown with green eyes,' and she details plaited hair, worn out clothes and manners both good and bad.

Although she is asked by residents not to take inventory in their community, Staebler insists on doing so. She visits family after family, describing the state of houses, particularly any bad smells or signs of dirt, and depicts few residents without racially explicit adjectives, for instance, calling one woman a 'broad negro mammy.' She notes that someone has children out of wedlock and mentions the backwards lettering on gravestones in the village's cemetery. When residents request that she not photograph them, she ignores them, citing their superstitious fears of the camera and noting the 'suspicious hostility in their black eyes.'[64]

Staebler frequently appropriates residents' voices, transcribing their black vernacular with her own gratuitous interpretation and spelling of accents and sounds.[65] As if to solidify the community's responsibility for its own plight, she ends with quotations from a black man who compliments whites and asserts that the community suffers no racism.

Staebler's work is meant to engage the white middle-class reader,[66] to bring the shocking reality of this slice of 'degenerate Africa' within white, Western civilization, into the mind and home of this subject. The author consistently stresses her own bravery and daring. She mentions entering the community despite warnings, going back after a less than welcoming reception by some residents, returning day after day, and persisting in her questioning and photography against the people's will. Staebler emerges (though, in her own view, just barely) safe with her story in hand. In the last line she describes a group of angry children who again refuse to be photographed and shout warnings and threats as she leaves.

While not usually described in such grandiose terms, local news articles betray similar journeys. Reporters were consistently preoccupied with documenting Africville's slum-like conditions. Frank Doyle, the executive editor of Halifax's local daily newspaper, wrote frequently about the situation in Africville in ways that suggest he observed the community a great deal. He describes the community's appearance, noting, for example, 'the shacks into which people are crowded,' and elsewhere writes: 'Yesterday at one time, a dozen or more scavengers were at work. How many were engaged in this occupation through the day, no one knows, but there was much coming and going ... They find many things – a barrel of over-salted meat occasionally, sometimes fruit is discovered – a real prize.'[67] Elsewhere, Doyle writes, of material salvaged from the dump, 'much of that waste is converted into litter scattered through the community.'[68] (In later interviews,

Africville residents noted that the majority did not depend on the dump, and most used it only occasionally.)[69] These depictions are often accompanied by appeals to the city to expedite Africville's eradication.

While simply home for the black community, for whites, Africville signified many things – a slum, a repository for the waste of society, a site of danger and degeneracy, a social problem, an object of pity and attempted rescue, and, I would argue, a mirror in which the white community saw its superiority reflected.

Consonant with statements in the *Relocation Report*, some white Haligonians have described informally the place Africville held in their imaginations as youths. One acquaintance described the curiosity in their gaze as 'treating it like going to the zoo, really … ' A black non-resident, in an interview with the report's authors, stated, 'people of all sorts used to go to Africville. It had a kind of attraction because it was kind of weird; no law enforcement. One went out there at one's own risk. It really was the other side of the tracks.'[70] A city official described a high school practice of driving to Africville, turning out the head-lights, and then turning them on to watch the rats run.[71] Other out-siders, both black and white, noted the common practice of going to Africville for 'women and alcohol';[72] many mentioned only the bootlegging, partying, and drinking for which the area was reknowned.[73] It was also reported that prominent white citizens some-times ventured into the community and were assisted by residents when they got drunk.

As a space of so-called deviant activity, Africville offered both escape and risk for the white community. The community's reputation as a wild and dangerous place is thought to have developed in its last two decades, following the Second World War. This is attributed to an influx of transients and squatters who increased the level of bootleg-ging, drinking and fighting, giving the media a chance to condemn all of Africville for these activities. Researchers Clairmont and Magill note that the crime rate in Africville was not particularly high and prison sentences were uncommon,[74] and no measure has been made of the prominence of drinking, bootlegging, or partying in Africville com-pared with other communities. And even though it appears that white people took part in deviant activities in Africville, the stigma remained with those who lived there, while whites returned unscathed to their respectable spaces.

Clairmont and Magill posit that the dominant community tolerated deviant activity in Africville due to the racial stigma that made it seem only natural. They write, 'Such indulgence by the authorities reflects not liberality but, rather, a view that the minority people are "different"'[75] Thus, the black community was seen as a space outside the law. Conversely, it was denied police services, reflecting how bodies belonging to the spaces of degeneracy are already outside the domain of rights and protection.[76] Participation by dominant group members in degenerate activity is uninterrogated.

Stories of transgression are enlightening for many reasons. They speak to the fascination and fear that underlie the venture into racialized space. They both mark that space as Other and document its character, often in a kind of detail that betrays at least as much about the subject of observation as the object. These stories comprise a widespread societal pedagogy that is essential to the making of spaces and subjects as immeasurably different and unequal.

Negating Knowledge

[When they] held out integration like some kind of Holy Grail, we told them we weren't sure exactly what integration could do for us as a community. And the fact that we would raise doubts about it – well, that kind of shocked 'em.

Charles Saunders[77]

I have so far discussed dominant discourses around blacks' criminality, cultural pathology, backwardness, and degeneracy. I have attempted to outline ways in which whites studied, documented, and policed black communities, delineated their outsider status and marked their inferiority. But something else, too, was fundamental to the process of Africville's removal. Throughout the period of knowledge production in question, writers, officials, and experts relentlessly discredited black residents' knowledge about their own situation, their views, perceptions, and, at the most basic level, their capacity for rationality. Racialization, then, requires not only the creation and mobilization of knowledge, but the disavowal of existing knowledge that does not support dominant assumptions about what is right, true, or necessary.

As the earlier quote conveys, whites were caught quite off guard by displays of black agency or critical thought. Frances Henry concludes that blacks have no sense of identity, 'no ultimate value system with which to guide their lives,' and lack the political awareness of their U.S. counterparts. She expresses surprise that people understand provincial and federal politics and have opinions about them.[78]

The report on the *Condition of the Negroes* calls into question the very intellectual capability of blacks. In one section, it addresses their 'educability,' illustrating that the central question is whether or not, and to what degree, blacks can be educated at all. The authors conclude that biological race does not *seem* to influence intelligence,[79] and place greater emphasis on socio-economic factors in educational attainment. However, they still draw on racial narratives in concluding that, without outside assistance, black children, like poor whites, will be destined to repeat the 'limitations and disabilities' of their parents.[80]

Speaking specifically about Africville, the author of a social work thesis about Africville's relocation suggests the illiteracy and unintelligence of residents as the reasons for their failed relations with the city. He attributes flaws within the relocation program to residents' lack of comprehension, illiteracy, hostility toward the city, and attempts to cling to their former ways of life within their new communities. He notes that relocation problems can be overcome only through their 'rehabilitation,'[81] suggesting that their failure to understand reason prevents blacks from proper submission to white authority.

White discourses also consistently discredit claims or examples of racism. The report *The Condition of the Negroes*, for instance, pays lip service to some discrimination in employment, but the authors also speculate that blacks perceive discrimination where it does not exist. An article in *Maclean's* magazine explains an example of 'so-called' discrimination in Halifax as simply stemming from merchants' fears that white customers will avoid their stores if they hire black workers. The author, Susan Dexter, quotes studies demonstrating that blacks would be accepted more easily than they perceived in Halifax rental housing (while local blacks explained that the rents were so high in the areas cited that landlords could afford to speak liberally, never having to worry about blacks affording their housing).[82]

Another report discusses blacks' reported experiences of harassment in Halifax, such as being followed and monitored in stores, difficulty renting apartments, verbal racial slurs, and an example of physical assault. This article, entitled 'Walking Black through Halifax,'[83] is written by a white journalist who accompanies and interviews blacks in their everyday lives. Allegedly attempting to understand the feeling of being black in a white dominated society, he continually questions and doubts their accounts of racism and attributes the incidents to benign factors or dismisses them as paranoia. (In contrast to Frances Henry, who suggests that they are ignorant of racism.)

Residents' claims to their community in Africville are often ridiculed through discourses that infantilize them and reposition their views as wrongful perceptions. Experts often imply that if only residents could understand the reasoning behind the appropriation of their community, they would be more accepting. They also maintain that the city has been patient and generous, waiting for Africville residents to come around and allowing them special privileges and opportunities. Further, dominant authors express alarm and frustration that residents are not grateful for the city's intervention. A news article states:

> some spokesmen for the Negro people who occupy the shacks say the municipal authorities have more than a usual responsibility in dealing with the community. The latter tolerated, if they did not actually encourage … construction; they allow scavenging on the dump, an income-yielding occupation that holds many in the area. They even ignore a resolution passed Nov. 15, 1932, by City Council. Concerning the dump, then in another nearby place, it said that 'the city engineer be requested to instruct his man in charge of the dump not to allow anyone to remove anything from the dump.'[84]

This report, by Frank Doyle, also remarks that city council has 'overlooked' the building of homes in the community, for which permits would normally be required (a different slant on the fact that requests for permits by Africville residents had been routinely denied). The author rewrites denial and neglect as patience and tolerance in a tone that infantilizes Africville residents by humouring their practices. For instance, when describing how residents use dump materials to improve their homes, Doyle writes 'improving' in quotation marks, and cites waste materials as 'riches.' Another article reports on a fire in Africville, stating that three children were killed when their 'home' burned down.[85] A news headline, 'Africville Residents Want "Promises" Kept,'[86] also suggests that the promises in question are merely a skewed perception by Africville people.

The *Maclean's* article by Susan Dexter reports city councillors' shock that people have accused them of neglecting Africville, and that their generosity has been met with distrust, fear, and reluctance to move. While it is not clear if the author feels this shock is warranted, her portrayal of Africville itself discredits the community's cause. She cites 'negro apathy' as the culprit that has prevented compensation for residents in the past, and that allowed their unsafe conditions to prevail.

Dexter consistently portrays the city as generous, specifying the unnecessary $500 compensation offered to residents who are 'not owed a cent.'[87]

The media upholds a notion of the city's generosity at almost every turn. Speaking of the final decision on forced relocation, another author states, 'Unfortunately, even the latest plan, which appears to many Haligonians to be both just and humane, is running into some opposition – from the residents of Africville.' The same article suggests that moves made to demolish Africville over time have been made 'difficult' by residents, but congratulates the city on managing the tasks despite this. The author suggests there is a widespread (and misplaced) sympathy for their plight: 'It is going to take some courage for the aldermen to move persons who do not want to be moved – persons almost everyone feels have been pushed around already – even when it will surely be for their own good.'[88]

News reports, urban planning, and academic studies from midcentury Nova Scotia frequently reiterate the same word – *hostile* – to describe the responses of the black community generally and Africville residents in particular. The report *The Condition of the Negroes* warns that unskilled intervention may be met with 'hostility' rather than 'gratitude.' *Maclean's* author Staebler describes the 'hostility' among residents when she continues to study and photograph them against their will. This label is echoed in a later *New York Times* article.[89] Frances Henry notes participants' hostility to some of her questions. As we will see in chapter 5, this accusation runs strongly into the present as well. White officials, media, and decision makers consistently charge an inexcusable rage when blacks dare to question their entitlement to observe, to report, to *know* the Other, and to know what is best.

Conclusion

Although the accounts explored here were dominant and lead to clear, profound consequences, I do not want to leave the impression that no counter-discourses existed. There was a growing and active black-led movement against racism in Nova Scotia, which was concerned with poor housing, poverty, and unemployment, as well as day-to-day forms of discrimination. Smaller and alternative newspapers and journals showed increased attention to poverty and racism, particularly during the early 1970s. *The Fourth Estate*, in 1972, reported on a housing conference organized at the grassroots level to educate non-specialists about land development and public housing conditions. Around this time, a magazine called *The Black Insight* was also launched in Halifax as a forum for black writers and their politics. As part of a network of groups across Canada, their work took a radical approach in dealing with personal and social issues simultaneously, and emphasized issues such as the lack of black history in school curricula and the negative portrayal of blacks in the media.

Clairmont and Magill, in 1970, note the increasing influence of the Nova Scotia Association for the Advancement of Coloured People (NSAACP), and report on progress throughout the 1960s in the areas of housing rights, professional training, school integration, and desegregation in public areas. In this work they also refute several theories that attribute the continued oppression of Nova Scotian blacks to alleged apathy or the competitive 'leveling' noted earlier by Henry. They critique assertions by historian Robin Winks that Canadian blacks have historically failed to understand the racism they face, and to organize around it. In a recent thesis, Sheridan Hay documents black agency throughout Nova Scotian history, arguing that a tradition of protest has always existed, though disavowed and often overridden by the dominant society.[90] Judith Fingard, too, documents black activism around school desegregation in the late nineteenth century.[91]

Dominant discourses, however potent, are rarely completely uncontested. However, critical thinkers, black and white alike, faced a powerful and authoritative history composed of deeply entrenched racial knowledge and near-impermeable fictions of black community. The sources discussed here comprise the main racial narratives produced by whites about Africville and black Nova Scotians generally. They were key and widely distributed instruments of education about these communities. The Stephenson report, for instance, was widely circulated and is often quoted in news articles, theses, and books about Africville. The report *The Condition of the Negroes of Halifax City* had far-reaching influence, constituting a key educational tool. Many professors from various disciplines were acknowledged for their assistance or comments in this work, and eight masters theses were produced by social work students who conducted research for the main project and then wrote about their findings. The *Halifax Region Housing Survey* resulted in a new course at Dalhousie University to educate students as to the 'values inherent in community planning.'[92] The survey's authors revised maps and prepared reports from this project for medical and law students, to aid in their rotations through the community. *Maclean's* has long been Canada's most popular and influential news magazine. Following the Second World War, it had a Canadian circulation of about 275,000, and its international issue reached almost one million people.[93] Africville's story also received coverage in the national news and regular coverage in Nova Scotia's major daily papers.

As will be seen more acutely in the following chapter, the discourses produced in these works had a direct impact on Africville. For instance, Albert Rose, an expert in social work and welfare from the University of Toronto,[94] drew heavily on these reports and articles in recommending Africville's destruction. The city government called Rose to Halifax in November of 1963, in order to review the Africville decision, indicate possible alternatives, and suggest whether further research would be useful. He reported that he felt city officials and experts were already well informed about the Africville situation, and his ensuing recommendations directly reflected the existing white discourses.[95]

Knowledge produced about poor and racialized communities reaches a broad public audience. As well as permeating government policy, it is picked up in influential professions such as education, law, social work, and medicine, and is conveyed widely to the general public in news reports. Such knowledge engages the nation in the expression of a set of normative values. Those in positions to influence outcomes are overwhelmingly from groups to whom these values will seem natural and beneficial. Foucault's 'regimes of truth' congeal in the racial discourses surrounding the slum. This logic is upheld as the slum does see more obvious strife, and that struggle is reported in particularly visible ways. Race, place, class, gender, sexuality, morality, degeneracy, and rationality all converge to outline the internal logic by which constructed knowledges and their effects are self-perpetuating.

The people of Africville were fundamentally, discursively, and materially defeated from the outset. There was no way that black people in Nova Scotia could win: When they failed to speak or were unheard, they were said to be docile and apathetic. When they did protest the invasion of their communities, they were called paranoid and hostile. When they analysed their oppression, they were assumed to invent or exaggerate it, yet when they failed to see racism, they were criticized for their ignorance. When they questioned the white-defined solutions imposed on them, they were called irrational. When they rejected these arrangements, they were labelled ungrateful. These are some of the most extreme and far reaching technologies of racism – to deny people their rationality, their ability to think, to speak, to object, is ultimately to deny their humanity.

4 Razing Africville: Fusing Spatial Management and Racist Discourse

If people in the southern U.S. treated Negroes as well as we do in Halifax, they would have no racial problem. And you can quote me on that.

Halifax mayor, John E. Lloyd, 1962[1]

The destruction of a racialized community is a tremendous project. It demands that multiple discourses operate to construct a dominant understanding, or official story, of the problem in need of solving. It demands that the place and the people in it be illustrated, through these discourses, in particular ways, and that those images be reflected in the landscape. It requires a solid foundation of history, throughout which social relations have come to reflect a common sense knowledge about the differences between people, between races, and between communities.

With a sense of the racial discourses in operation prior to Africville's destruction, it is possible to think more critically about the technologies of spatial management that they enabled. The incitement to organize and to 'read' space in a racialized manner infuses those discourses as well: in short, race requires space in order to make sense. But the underlying impetus to study how this comes to be is not simply to trace an interesting conceptual entanglement; it is to better understand how its consequences play out on the ground. What do racial knowledge and spatial practices, combined, enable people to *do*? And how, then, do those people understand and explain their *doing*? This chapter provides a close look at the process of Africville's destruction, mapping the intricate and deliberate planning process among city officials and their associates.

My analysis relies often on the 1971 *Africville Relocation Report*, by Donald Clairmont and Dennis Magill. These researchers were commissioned by the Nova Scotia Department of Public Welfare, in conjunction with the Department of National Health and Welfare, to conduct a detailed study of the relocation program, and to evaluate its success. They carried out their study at the project's tail end, interviewing residents, city officials, planners, the relocation social worker, and various scholars.

Clairmont and Magill had extensive access to the process and its key actors. They were able to document city council meetings, for instance, and then obtain different participants' opinions as to what had occurred in them. They obtained first person accounts of meetings in Africville about the future move. Their report has been published as a book which is now in its third edition, and Clairmont has gone on to collaborate closely with the Africville community on commemorative work.

The *Relocation Report* is extremely thorough; its detail far surpasses any other source of written information about Africville's destruction. I have both drawn on it and departed from it. I have also drawn on news accounts of events, retrospective works by black writers, official letters and minutes of meetings, and visual representations of Africville's history at the Nova Scotia Black Cultural Centre. Many of the original sources of data I have cited, such as news articles and planning reports, are also referred to in the *Relocation Report*, although my reading of them reflects my particular theoretical and analytic concerns, which, of course, emerged at a very different point in time with respect to Africville's end. What this chapter offers is both a detailed examination of the process of destruction, and a new reading that considers and critiques its dominant interpretations.

The Destruction of Africville

Encroachment

It was early in Africville's life that the provincial and Intercolonial Railway began to infringe on the community. A petition from William Brown of Africville, dated 21 March 1860, requests compensation for land expropriated by the city six years earlier,[2] and an 1855 report states that several families had been moved but had yet to be compensated. In some cases, railway trustees provided nearby land for relocatees but did not sign it over to them for five years.[3] By 1901, the city had forced five families to move to make way for more railway tracks; before long, several sets of tracks had been built through the centre of Africville, meaning residents were forced to cross them to visit neighbours or attend school.[4]

Besides the noise, pollution, and danger of the railways, Africville had soon to contend with a nearby prison, an infectious diseases hospital, the nearby dump, and the city's night soil.[5] The municipality built a trachoma hospital in the Africville area after other city residents complained about its proposed proximity to their own homes, requesting that it be isolated on the outskirts.[6] Halifax, by 1907, had purchased properties on all sides of Africville. This placed the city in a good position to bargain with manufacturers wishing to expand; this expansion, in turn, produced more waste and in some cases required additional railway construction. In response to a growing need for cheap labour, many Africville men worked on the construction of rail lines, and others gathered the night soil from Halifax, bringing it 'home' with them.[7] Thus the relationship of Africville people to those who encroached on their space became one of dependence, with Africville hosting the city's dirt, relying on the meagre wages offered, and having to fight for compensation when its employers destroyed its homes. Meanwhile, Halifax expanded its industry and transportation, and contained much of its waste in a racial slum on the outskirts of the city while avoiding the expense of providing services to those who lived there.

The construction of industry in this area contributed to further spatial class and race divisions as former white north-end residents flocked to the southern neighbourhoods to avoid the blight and decay of the north. With a conscious agenda to expand the north end as an industrial site, the city government refused improvements in Africville's living conditions, saying that the land was slated for industrial use. City council minutes suggest that municipal officials had long planned Africville's future as an industrial zone. The city engineer, in 1915, stated this intent, adding 'we may be obliged in the future to consider the interest of the industry first.'[8] However, as plans to take over the land were not to become official policy until the 1960s, Africville was forced to live in an uncertain state, increasingly endangered by fire hazards and contaminated water, while officials dodged questions and avoided head-on confrontation of the issue. Other than the occasional rumour of mass dislocation, residents had few glimpses of what they might face, and neither time nor resources to prepare.

In the decades leading up to Africville's destruction, various negotiations between the city and industries took place over the use of its land, none of which involved discussion with residents themselves. Small plants and industries in the area continued to operate or shift hands, and the city relocated its dump even more centrally on Africville land, with no consultation with residents.[9] The city maintained a steadfast control over its Africville area properties, refusing offers of purchase from private citizens. When Africville's pastor requested land to rebuild the church, city council members agreed, on the advice of the city engineer, to lease the land on the condition that it be allowed to revoke the space and destroy the church 'promptly' if need be. They also rented unserviced lots to several Africville families, continuing to collect rental income in the interim period while planning the appropriation of the land. For a period, there was discussion of 'redeveloping' the area as a residential site. A 1945 Civic Planning Commission report recommended the removal of Africville, the city prison and the abattoir, in order to build 'a most desirable residential section.'[10] However, council adhered, in principle, to its industrial plans.

Other uses of Africville land were occasionally approved and then deserted, as if council were paying lip service to other ideas while never seeing them through. In 1948, after a city-wide rezoning, plans were officially approved for the extension of a water line into Africville, but were never put into effect. In the early 1950s, the city manager presented a report to council involving plans for the movement of Africville people to a nearby area, just to the southwest of the community's current site. This plan budgeted for water lines, sewerage, proper lighting, and the construction of sidewalks, curbs, and gutters. It provided for large lots on which two-storey houses would be built and sold to residents at prices believed possible for them. This plan was accepted by council, but was also never implemented.

Council's reasons for the abandonment of this and the 1948 water line proposal are not offered in the *Relocation Report* or elsewhere, to my knowledge. They seem only to have quietly joined the city's proverbial graveyard of promises, existing and upcoming, where Africville was concerned. Again, they had been drawn in the absence of negotiation with Africville residents. Government officials continually discussed Africville as a 'problem' that they would solve largely amongst themselves and with the supporting advice of outside experts. They proceeded with invitations to Canadian National Railways, the National Harbours Board, and the Port of Halifax Commission to participate in detailed planning around the development of the 'Industrial Mile.'[11]

At the same time, the two decades leading up to Africville's end saw many changes in the social structure of the village. According to both residents and researchers, a number of transient people arrived after the Second World War, bringing with them more drinking, bootlegging, and crime.[12] Those not indigenous to Africville were seen by outsiders as representative of the community, and their deviant behaviour became a generalized assumption on the part of other Haligonians. Given the pre-existing racial discourses about Africville as a slum area, the lack of services and, now, some social fragmentation, the city saw the time as ripe for the community's removal. City officials, armed with the integration rhetoric of the day, the various urban renewal studies, and much research about black communities, could justify clearing what most whites considered a filthy and degenerate racial slum.

By the mid-1950s, council was clear that it would soon expropriate Africville lands. It had acquired one area in Africville by 1957, and had released the Stephenson report, echoing plans for industrial development and concerns about community viability, in the same year. From this period on, city officials appear to have spent much time discussing, in the words of one alderman, 'a great urgency in securing title to these lands.'[13] The plan to build an Industrial Mile was soon adopted and eventually incorporated into the greater North Shore Development Plan. By 1962, this agenda included plans for an expressway running through the Africville site, a certain amount of industrial development, a housing section constructed on the city prison's lands[14] with a primary school in the former prison building, and ample recreational facilities. In this plan, released to the press in February of 1962, the removal of Africville was said to be slated for the spring of that year. Clairmont and Magill, however, document that no concrete relocation plans were drawn until 1963. This apparent incongruence over the nature and timing of plans seems to foreshadow the overall tenor of decision making.

The Pretence of Consultation

> The only solution to this problem was to get the people out of there and into something that more approximated a normal way of life.
>
> Albert Rose[15]

The Housing Policy and Review Committee, in 1961, recommended the establishment of a new department to oversee the demolition of Africville. The Development Department, which would administer urban renewal programs, was formed a few months later. Development officer Robert Grant began his term with a focus on three major areas: the downtown redevelopment, Uniacke Square – a housing project for relocated residents, and Africville itself. Interviewed several years later by Clairmont, Grant reported that he had perceived three possible directions from which to begin planning in Africville: he could undertake another survey, he could compose a report without knowing anything about Africville, or he could attempt to learn about Africville 'in an indirect way, without getting down to the real individual problems ... but to define generally what the situation was in some more meaningful way than by rumour.'[16] Feeling that the first option would be fruitless and would 'create more hostility,' and the second irresponsible, he undertook to learn about Africville indirectly. Grant's plan consisted of scheduling 'several discussions with a young gentleman who had been a resident of Africville as a youngster and pretty well knew ... what their circumstances were, not necessarily up to date, but generally the situation.'[17] After these conversations, with one former resident who had lived there only as a child, Grant wrote a report to city council describing the people and the conditions in Africville, and recommending its demolition 'despite the wishes of many of the residents.'[18]

Grant's report opens with the ubiquitous excerpt from the Stephenson report that begins, 'There is a little frequented part of the City, overlooking Bedford Basin, which presents an unusual problem for any community to face.'[19] Grant uses this summary of conditions and his own 'research' as the basis for his decisions. He foregrounds the legal machinery by which buildings could be ordered vacated and demolished, and land expropriated. He offers three options for policies toward Africville, including, for one, the plan to continue to do nothing. His second option is to use full statutory powers to remove the blight and to limit compensation to 'the absolute minimum required by law.' Third, the option he recommends – and which is thereafter quoted frequently – is to use statutory authority to 'remove the blight and, at the same time, temper justice with compassion in matters of compensation and assistance to the families affected.'[20] In this, the city is able to go beyond its official obligation, to remove Africville while appearing not only concerned but generous. Grant advises caution in making sure the gratuitous payments of $500 go only to 'deserving persons.' This would be determined based on their ability to obtain written proof from a minister (or other 'responsible person') attesting to occupancy of their homes for at least five years.[21] Despite his meagre research, Grant later told Clairmont and Magill that he had been determined to avoid 'rebuilding a coloured ghetto on the same land.'[22] He admitted that his reasons had been 'pretty primitive,' but did not elaborate.

Grant's Development Department Report was released to the *Mail Star* on 1 August 1962. One week later, nearly one hundred Africville people met with MLA Ahern from Halifax North, at his request, to discuss the proposed plans; they unanimously rejected the move. Residents, after years of petitioning for services and building permits for their community, again expressed their desire to improve the homes they owned according to city specifications.[23] Ahern was one of a few government officials sympathetic to their concerns and told the press he felt it unfair to take a home someone owned and replace it with one rented from someone else.[24]

The release of the report sparked a more intensive focus on organization around the impending relocation plan. However, activism had long been underway. Influenced by contact with the National Committee on Human Rights, some Africville residents formed a ratepayers association. In response to Africville residents' complaints about their inability to obtain building permits from the city, the National Committee's associate secretary advised more intensive organization of leadership in Africville, and sent a lawyer, Alan Borovoy, to meet with residents and city officials to study Africville's situation. His visit involved some research into the nature and level of racism in Halifax. He also encouraged internal initiative and was able to catalyse the Halifax Human Rights Advisory Committee (HHRAC) by introducing some key Africville leaders to city activists, both black and white, who showed interest in protecting residents' rights. However, Borovoy, like most social reformers of the time, stressed the importance of racial integration and opposed the rehabilitation of Africville as a community. When interviewed later for the Clairmont report, he admitted having had little knowledge of Africville upon his arrival and that he had perceived the community as a slum and its residents as 'squatters and transients.' Borovoy, who accepted that the community's destruction was inevitable, focused on the achievement of a fair deal for residents upon relocation, their successful integration into the rest of society, and the implementation of fair employment and accommodation legislation.[25]

The HHRAC, organized in the wake of Borovoy's visit, consisted of a core membership of ten people – four whites and six blacks – three of whom were from Africville. Other citizens attended various meetings at different times over the group's six-year existence, but in general, membership remained low. The group's mandate was to protect the interests of Africville people, to investigate alternative living accommodations, and to provide advice and technical information. All but one of the non-Africville members were proponents of racial integration. At no point was the group considered by Africville residents to represent their position; the Africville group members were not elected or appointed by community residents, and consultation with the community was practically nonexistent.[26] The HHRAC did, however, attempt to form a clearer picture of the city's intentions regarding Africville, and to discern their reasons for expropriating the land based on questions arising from meetings in Africville.

In HHRAC correspondence with Robert Grant, the development officer represents the city's mandate as principally humanitarian in nature, with the aim of improving living conditions for Africville people. He notes that redevelopment of the area in an 'orderly' way will be a secondary benefit. He also reminds residents that, had they not been historically 'unique' as a community, the lands would have been taken much earlier and the people left to fend for themselves.[27] The onset of this correspondence seemed to delineate a marked shift in the city's reasoning behind its relocation agenda – from industrial development to urban renewal for the purposes of integration. Although at times both reasons were cited, it became increasingly more common to hear about the appalling conditions in Africville and the need to establish a healthier way of life for the community. Industrial development, which was never achieved on a large scale, seemed to fall by the wayside once the integration discourses of the 1960s became more central.[28]

Meeting with the HHRAC following this correspondence, Grant consistently vetoed the committee's alternative suggestions for new housing. One member requested the investigation of building new homes in the north end that could be purchased, rather than public housing. When the development officer replied that there was no reasonable basis on which to subsidize homes, it was suggested they be built 'as an act of reparation.'[29] This, Grant replied, would require a policy decision beyond his responsibility. It appears that he did not propose the idea to council, and it went no further.

During this meeting, the HHRAC expressed concern that negotiations with landowners had begun to take place on an individual basis, rather than in an organized and consistent manner. Throughout the relocation period, it appears that the city's method of dealing with residents one-on-one contributed to the difficulties of organizing as a collective, and sometimes resulted in divisive suspicion and bitterness within the community. When Grant met with people in Africville shortly after the issue arose, he reported that residents had nothing to say and felt that the HHRAC members were the only ones who appeared 'disturbed' by the city's actions.[30]

In the meantime, following the release of Grant's document, the mayor accepted various reports from officials, including the city manager, city assessor, commissioner of works, commissioner of health and the public service commission.[31] He also considered the Dalhousie report, *The Conditions of the Negroes*, before calling an official meeting, at which the city unanimously accepted the destruction of Africville as a policy decision. When the HHRAC expressed outrage that neither they nor the people of Africville had been consulted about this decision, Mayor Lloyd replied that the meeting had been held only 'to set the machinery in motion to procure the views and wishes of the residents before a final decision is made by Council.' By this time, although a large portion of Africville's land had been expropriated, the city continued to collect tax money from residents living there. When this additional concern was raised, the mayor simply agreed that no further decisions would be made until residents' views had been fully considered. Despite this, city council met the very next day and adopted specific guidelines concerning the procedure of 'relocation.'[32]

While the HHRAC was not representative of the majority of Africville residents' desires, they did appear to put significant effort into researching alternatives to the city's plans. Over a period of about eighteen months, the committee explored options such as cooperative housing, condominiums, private homes, and the rehabilitation of Africville on site. Some were rejected by the city due to expenses, and the committee feared that cooperative arrangements would be impossible due to residents' low finances, skills, and employment levels.[33] Finding no apparent viable options, the committee consulted Albert Rose, from the University of Toronto,[34] whom the city had summoned as an expert housing consultant in 1963.

Rose told Clairmont and Magill that he spent no more than two hours in Africville, and described it as 'the worst urban appendage [he] had ever seen,' and 'a bottomless pit,' in which resource investment would be wasted.[35] The rest of his visit was spent interviewing five city officials, two social workers, and two university specialists, and speaking informally with other social work colleagues. Rose, like many other white 'experts,' was of the opinion that segregated housing was unthinkable, and discouraged Africville members of the HHRAC from pursuing federal or provincial funding to rebuild the community.

Rose conveyed to Africville residents that no more options lay open to them and that relocation was inevitable. He reported, in an interview with Clairmont and Magill, that residents had questioned him repeatedly, 'desperately clutching at last straws,' to find a way to save their community.[36] Despite this, his report to city council ('Report of a Visit to Halifax with Particular Respect to Africville') following the visit stated: 'The residents of Africville appear ready and to some extent eager to negotiate a settlement concerning the ultimate disposition of their community ... The leaders of the community readily admit that Africville is a slum, that it should be cleared and that it would long since have been cleared if the inhabitants were of a different racial background.'[37] Following this starkly false statement (also noted in the *Relocation Report*), Rose advised against a larger study of Africville. He stated that most of the necessary facts were already known to city officials, who he felt possessed a great understanding of conditions in Africville. While he admitted officials had had little direct contact with families in Africville and knew little about their kinship systems, basic attitudes, and social relationships, he reported that further survey would only delay the crucial process of relocation. Among his reasons for supporting full-scale demolition of the community, Rose wrote: 'Can a minority group be permitted to reconstitute itself as a segregated community at a time in our history, at a time in the social history of western industrialized urban nations when segregation either de jure (in law) or de facto (in fact) is almost everywhere condemned?'[38] Thus, by appropriating civil rights discourse and appealing to the views of many liberals who embraced it, Rose positioned any impetus to save Africville as primitive and racist. He proceeded with a detailed outline of recommendations to make the move, in his view, as painless as possible. They included the full-scale destruction of Africville between 1 April 1964 and 31 December 1966.

While Rose's report was seen as the linchpin in the Africville relocation, Albert Rose himself stated in retrospect that he had never considered his work to be a final or master plan and was surprised when the city treated it with such reverence. He was critical of the city for accepting only the aspects of his report that directly supported their agenda. However, both an HHRAC member and the development officer reported that they suspected Rose had been supportive of the city's decision before he ever visited Halifax. The media capitalized on this confirmation of the city's goals, providing wide coverage of the Rose report and the city's acceptance of it. Shortly after Rose's visit, the mayor was quoted as stating that the takeover 'would not in any way be breaking the wishes of the people there.'[39] Development officer Robert Grant clearly felt Rose to be an important outside source of confirmation of the city's existing intent, and HHRAC members also reported that his view dispelled doubts and confirmed their support for relocation.[40]

Within six weeks of the Rose report's release in December of 1963, Halifax city council formally accepted its recommendations. At this council meeting, Mayor Lloyd urged fast adoption so that legislation could be prepared in time for the next meeting of the Nova Scotia legislature. However, as a HHRAC member pointed out, the committee had only received copies of the report at the start of the meeting and had not had time to read it. Council agreed to take no further action until the committee had had this opportunity, but ordered the legislation drafted anyway. The HHRAC met immediately following this meeting and unanimously accepted the Rose report.[41]

Africville residents were called to a meeting after the HHRAC's approval of the report. At this meeting, after much explanation from the committee about the lack of alternatives, thirty-seven residents voted to accept the Rose report's recommendations. The HHRAC reported to city council the following day that the report had been accepted unanimously by the committee and by 90 per cent of Africville residents present. They neglected to mention that this 90 per cent consisted of only thirty-seven people, less than 10 per cent of the Africville population overall.

About one week later, the HHRAC approached council with some additional concerns of Africville residents. The mayor refused to engage with these issues, vaguely commenting that this was not the time to address specific points, but to establish 'broad principles.' He continued with general assurances that the city was prepared 'to look after the people' and do the best they could to make the transition work smoothly. When asked specifically by an elderly Africville woman about the problem of affording new homes, he responded only that the matter would be 'kept under continuous study' and that problems would be resolved as they transpired.[42] A motion was then passed to remove Africville within the time frame proposed by Albert Rose.

Demolition

> If you ever watched someone you love die slowly, day-by-day, hour-by-hour, then you know what it was like being in Africville during the relocation.
>
> Charles Saunders[43]

Taking up one of the suggestions in Rose's report, the city of Halifax appointed a social worker to oversee negotiations in housing arrangements and the transition of Africville residents to their new homes. Peter MacDonald took this position within the city Development Department in mid-1964 as the relocation was underway. Shortly after his arrival, development officer Robert Grant created a policy statement clarifying the relocation duties of both the department and the Africville subcommittee of city council. While the Development Department was to focus on broad, overarching issues, the subcommittee was to ensure the fulfilment of the city's duties to Africville residents. Provisions were made for compensation for both properties and relocation expenses. The Development Department was to be responsible for finding new homes and moving residents, as well as welfare assistance 'for such a period as appears necessary.'[44] The city was to provide rehabilitative programs in education and employment.

Development officer Robert Grant and the relocation social worker, Peter MacDonald, appear to have been the most influential players during the process of demolishing Africville. MacDonald was the only outsider to have regular contact with Africville people, and he was responsible for negotiating the terms of their compensation. MacDonald reported directly to Grant, who had ultimate authority on matters concerning the relocation program. Grant's role was described as that of 'supporting, justifying, and implementing City Council's Africville policy.' A member of city council's Africville subcommittee described his approach as concerned with the city's interests and designed to 'keep the costs down, get the thing cleaned up with as little controversy as possible, and therefore not letting too much information out.'[45] Another member of the subcommittee told Clairmont and Magill that he had sometimes felt uncomfortable with Grant's involvement and suspected some reports from Africville to have been 'whitewashed' in favour of the city. The solution to this concern, however, had been to insist that MacDonald, who was trusted, write the reports instead. This, of course, meant that the information remained within the same department, and was overseen by the same person.

Grant himself reported that the negotiation of each settlement took place between Peter MacDonald and the individual resident in question, was reported back to him, and was accepted or rejected by himself and MacDonald before it went on for broader committee approval.

In January of 1965, three middle-class black members of the HHRAC joined the Africville subcommittee in planning the relocation program. These members were purportedly chosen in order that it not look 'as if white people were doing the whole thing.'[46] From this point onward, the new committee of black organizers and council members became the body responsible for final decisions on Africville settlements recommended by MacDonald. The vast majority of cases received unanimous approval by the committee. Grant attributed this easy agreement to the fact that 'these were sensible people,'[47] and committee members themselves consistently viewed MacDonald as the expert who knew the community and understood the best solutions. After the subcommittee's approval, settlements were reviewed by the finance committee of council and then passed to city council, where they were rubber-stamped.

Some Africville community leaders expressed concern that the private nature of compensation agreements (negotiated almost solely between MacDonald and individual residents) contributed to an atmosphere of division and mistrust among residents. In many cases, residents were unaware of different settlements taking place and uncertain of the comparative fairness of their own deals. The city employed different methods of dealing with individuals; in some cases, they made settlements with older residents who were seen as community leaders, in the hope that other residents would follow their lead. In later interviews, some city officials admitted to offering better deals in initial negotiations to inspire other residents to consider leaving. Another official observed that the social assistance funds offered to residents by the relocation social worker were intended for this purpose.

> I think in many cases the effect was to soft-pedal or soft-pad the transitional period, to perhaps conceal from people really the full impact of the economic burden and so on which they would have to encounter, making the entire relocation more acceptable to the people and in many respects unrealistic because these funds were terminated with the termination of [the social worker's] employment.[48]

One elderly man, Aaron 'Pa' Carvery, held out longer than any others in his Africville home. Carvery later described to Clairmont and Magill how he was finally summoned to city hall by officials, who took him to a private room and offered him a suitcase full of cash.[49] When he refused to accept this, city officials raised the amount slightly and stated that the land would be taken whether or not he accepted the offer. When he asked that his house be moved to a nearby site, they initially agreed, but later changed their minds.

As Clairmont and Magill have ascertained, the overall tone of the city's plan left no room for either collective action or a cooperative approach. Likewise, subcommittee meetings were not open to residents as, according to city staff, the personal circumstances of residents being discussed were of a confidential nature, and they feared some residents might not treat them as such.

Settlements themselves were haphazard or set through informal precedent as the process unfolded. City council consistently avoided specific and detailed plans, sticking to benign, generalized statements such as 'taking care of people,' and 'for as long as it seems necessary.' The development officer noted that no guidelines existed because set values for the properties could never be legally justified. The relocation subcommittee claimed to have accepted Africville residents' stories of their land ownership in cases where proof was not available; however, most residents told Clairmont and Magill in surveys that they had never had contact with the subcommittee and were distrustful of the social worker. While Grant stated that the age, employment status, and the number of children in families were taken into account, another member of the subcommittee reported that 'character' and 'reputation' of residents were also important factors: 'Sometimes a Committee member would indicate that a certain fellow had a reputation as being very irresponsible, even though he had a family. If he got a grant of so much money, it would end up back in the provincial coffers via the liquor store, or something like that.'[50]

Grant's own view of Africville undoubtedly imbued his definition of undeserving citizens. He referred to Africville as a slum made up of shiftless people who prevailed mainly through their 'common misery.' He expressed both class- and race-based disdain for the lower orders in general, and stated about Africville, 'They had a tendency to live for today, and not worry about the consequences. I suppose it is not unlike some of the mining towns … You talk to a group of miners, you know, you say, "Why do you do this?" And they say, "We like it," and they live for today.'[51] Such judgment seems particularly ironic in light of the city's overwhelming failure to instigate any long-range plan themselves.

While some residents received above market value for their homes and land, many, who could not demonstrate clear title, received 'moral claim' payments of $500. Furniture allowances were offered, but when the city learned of some cases in which these funds had been used for other expenses, they insisted on holding the money and having furniture stores bill them directly for the purchases. While other services, such as legal and real estate advice, were ostensibly provided for residents, most residents surveyed were unaware of these and less than 15 per cent had used them. This seems tied to the extremely low level of communication between residents and both their alleged allies, the Halifax Human Rights Advisory Committee (HHRAC), and the city itself. Clairmont and Magill also found that Africville residents, even when made aware of these options, had been actively discouraged from using them, as the social worker was positioned as the only trustworthy source of assistance. Without any alternative contacts or resources, most fell back upon his guidance. In the words of Aaron 'Pa' Carvery: 'The City gave the Africville people no deal at all. Some were put into places far worse than what they left. Also, when people lived in Africville, they were not on welfare ... now, practically everyone is on welfare and in debt because of high rents and the cost of living ... I never did like charity, it robs a man of something.'[52]

In total, the city of Halifax paid out just under $608,000 in the process of removing Africville, including the cost of the church, in addition to waiving $20,600 in hospital and tax bills.[53] The projected cost of the process in 1962 had been between $40,000 and $70,000. The estimated cost of providing the community with streets, services, and new homes on a nearby site had been in the vicinity of $80,000.[54] Despite the fact that most residents continued to live in poverty, the city has long maintained that because they went far beyond their expected budget, they were empathetic and generous. This claim, however, discounts the fact that they grossly miscalculated the cost – it was a mistake, not a magnanimous act. The claim also fails to acknowledge that this settlement figure includes welfare payments that were necessary as a product of relocation, and that the waived bills included tax monies charged on properties that received no city services. Further, the majority of welfare payments were the product of a cost-sharing program between the local, provincial, and federal governments. The city's expenditures comprised approximately 25 per cent of the full cost.[55] On the whole, monies spent were the result of Halifax having refused its responsibilities in Africville for over one hundred years. An understanding of compensation can no more be divorced from history than one of forced dislocation itself.

A 1991 documentary film, *Remember Africville*, makes clear how the psychological effect of witnessing a slow and unpredictable decay of one's community remains a potent memory in the minds of former residents. One man speaks of coming home from school as a child to find that the church had been bulldozed and running to tell his mother, who had also been unaware of the plan; another describes never knowing when a nearby home might disappear. Physical danger was also a tangible fear; one resident remembers being inside a shed where he and his childhood friends frequently played when the city began bulldozing the building.[56] Peter Edwards, a leader in the Africville community and a member of the HHRAC, reported that the city had threatened to bulldoze people out if they were not cooperative in moving on their own.[57]

The move itself occurred gradually, with the community slowly disintegrating around those who remained – as one city alderman told a reporter, 'the bulldozer is there almost before the ink on the agreement dries.'[58] The emotional impact of this imposed decay has been noted as a further catalyst that worked in the city's favour to speed up the departures of some residents. As housing in the Halifax area was scarce, Africville people were frequently forced to wait for months after settling with the city before a unit became available. Often this meant living temporarily in another area slated for demolition. When moving companies refused to enter the community, the city sent garbage trucks to collect the people's belongings.

While some residents were able to afford their own homes in Halifax or outlying areas, the majority went to public housing projects – most commonly Uniacke Square in the city's north end. Although most people had owned their homes in Africville, less than one third remained homeowners after the move.[59] Forced to pay rent and other new expenses for the first time in their lives, the meagre settlements many had received from the city were spent quickly. Levels of unemployment remained high, and the number of those requiring welfare payments quadrupled.[60] While some follow-up programs were announced by the city, few were put into effect, and resident participation in these dwindled. Essentially, the end of the relocation saw the end of what little city assistance had been available at all.

Not the End

In mid-1967, MacDonald's term as the relocation social worker ended. He exited by sending a letter to each former resident, abruptly stating that they should contact the city welfare office when they required assistance in the future. This presented an acute crisis, as the welfare director had an entirely different perspective on several counts. First, the welfare director claimed he had never been consulted about this shift of responsibility; MacDonald had not once approached him or forewarned him of the notices he had sent to Africville residents. Second, he had been opposed to the Rose report and the community's demolition from the beginning, and felt the city should have provided for the specific needs of relocatees, which did not meet the regular criteria of welfare funds.[61] Another problem arose in that the duration of payments had not been made clear to Africville people, nor, it seems, within council itself. Similar to the vague 'official' answers on other issues, the development officer claimed they had merely warned relocatees that welfare 'would not be available indefinitely.'[62]

With a lack of definitive plans, dwindling financial compensation, abandonment by the relocation social worker, and the end of the HHRAC and the Africville subcommittee, dislocated Africville people were left to their own resources. City officials, in interviews, stated that they had expected the provincial government to take responsibility for follow-up programs. MacDonald had purportedly sent a letter recommending such follow-up to council, which was approved but never instituted. How this matter, approved only by city council, was supposed to engage provincial government support is not explained. Rather, it seems that all involved in administrative positions assumed another department was looking after the post-relocation recommendations, or at least they claimed this assumption when questioned as to their own inaction. HHRAC members explained that they, too, had assumed follow-up was taking place after their disbandment, and that MacDonald had left with a long-term plan in place to assist relocatees.[63]

After some months of floundering, realizing no one else had taken responsibility, the city established a Social Planning Department under the direction of a social worker, Harold Crowell. This department established a follow-up program, to be directed by Alexa McDonough,[64] also a social worker. The program first engaged in meetings and discussions with residents and other concerned citizens in an attempt to establish the gravity of the situation. They found Africville relocatees had incurred an enormous debt load due to their neglected needs and unpreparedness for increased living expenses. Funds were petitioned from the provincial government, with some supplementation by the city, and the Seaview Credit Union was established to deal with debt payments. This union was largely unsuccessful, however, as unstable employment, inflation, illnesses, or other difficulties prevented many residents from meeting their financial commitments. Africville residents also tended to distrust the institution as another city-sponsored project.[65]

At the same time, the Africville Action Committee, composed of former residents, was formed to demand compensation and the fulfilment of promises made by the city.[66] They brought to light three major promises that had been broken: one year of free rent in their new accommodations, a furniture allowance of $1000 per family, and a review of the Africville land values, from which any adjustment should be placed in a trust fund for former residents.[67] According to these residents, revaluation and compensation for expropriation of land had been promised until 1987. The latter promise, however, had only been indicated verbally by the Africville subcommittee and the finance committee, and was not legally binding to the city. The mayor claimed that the former promises, of rent payment and furniture allowance, were not recorded in council minutes. The majority of residents, it was determined, had received free rent for about two months only;[68] one reported having been sent to a welfare line when he requested further rent payments.[69] The furniture allowance had not been administered fully. Some residents were later billed directly by furniture stores; these residents, when unable to access city funds, had no choice but to pay. Some residents held signed letters from the city clerk pledging city assistance with mortgages or other bills in the case of illness, disability, or unemployment, and these had not been honoured. The social worker later confirmed that such letters had been sent, and also that the payment of furniture money and the review of land values had been valid claims.[70] Other residents were angry at the ignorance of city officials as to promises made in their own homes by the social worker or other officials.

Overall, various administrators appear to have promised different methods and amounts of compensation and support at different times, on an informal, individual basis. Some were signed, some were simply verbal agreements. Amendments to the Rose report, which had been demanded on behalf of residents by the HHRAC, seemed to have been lost in bureaucratic chaos, and the city allowed the follow-up programs discussed in the report, such as employment and training, to quietly recede.

Dispersed through a predominantly white community, Africville blacks faced intense hostility in several ways. In one case, a white neighbour is reported to have begun a petition to oppose the entrance of a black family, while another black relocatee was threatened.[71] One man received a letter composed of words clipped from magazines, warning that his new house would be burned down if he and his family moved in. It was signed, simply, 'from the white people of Hammonds Plains.'[72] Some were rejected from public housing by the Housing Authority due to 'unsuitability,' which appeared to have stood for different notions of acceptable family and home life. Even the *Mail Star*, which tended to report positively on Africville's destruction, noted Peter MacDonald's statement that some landlords had been concerned their white tenants would not like new black neighbours.[73] Clairmont and Magill write, 'the fluid social structure of Africville was at variance with the cut-and-dried style acceptable to the housing authority. Africville residents had a tradition of extended families, consisting of several generations and quasi-extended family household formation.'[74] In the words of the relocation social worker:

> The Africville people generally were always able to make room for one more. By that I am particularly thinking of the older people, the grandfather, and the grandmother, and the aunt, and the uncle who were elderly. These people were looked after ... When they were thinking of moving out [relocating] ... this was one of the factors that they thought about first, that they would have to provide a room for so-and-so.[75]

Africville people were judged against white middle-class family values, and dominant racial discourses. In line with the urban planners' concerns of social disorder, crime, and the discipline of children, Africville residents were pressured to abide by the narrow lifestyle definitions imposed by their new spatial arrangements. For instance, there is evidence that some single Africville mothers were required to marry the fathers of their children in order to obtain money for furniture.[76] Various single women with families were forced to accept welfare for the first time, whereas they had previously survived by living in extended family homes or with parents who were able to help them. One family reported having to send several children to live with friends or relatives to adapt to the financial and spatial constraints of relocation.[77] One woman was unable to afford the added rental cost of allowing her teenage grandson to live with her as they had planned.[78] Various families reported grief at the break-up of homes that had included extended kin, boarders, or friends. In only two cases were large families maintained after the move, and it became common for households to survive by taking in boarders or welfare recipients they didn't know, for which they received a 'guardian payment.'

Clairmont and Magill point out the irony of families giving up close kinship ties in exchange for sharing their limited space with strangers in an act of social service. At the same time, the government was forced to make up, through welfare dollars, many of the costs of living previously met through the sharing of resources and space in homes Africville residents owned. Indeed, the design of the new housing projects was intended to compress families into a mould of middle class, 'respectable' dwelling. In response to the 'unsuitability' of some residents for their new surroundings, the city placed them in old, decrepit, and unsafe quarters, many of which were condemned shortly after they arrived.[79] The Social Planning Department proposed plans for housekeeping courses that would prepare them to care for a public housing unit and, while a full program was not put into effect, two families were assisted in 'upgrading their housekeeping standards.'[80]

Meanwhile, the local press continued to emphasize the need for faster dispersal of Africville, and featured stories in which residents were depicted as content and satisfied.[81] The relocation social worker was cited in the local paper as stating, 'there is every indication that the younger generation will become completely self-sufficient in its new habitat beyond the railroad tracks and the city dump.'[82] Efforts to fight these dominant images comprised an uphill battle. While the Africville Action Committee was initially successful in bringing some problems to light, it was made up of former residents who had little internal cohesion and no external advice or support. With residents spread out over the city and province, most struggling under severe poverty, it was difficult to maintain initiative in fighting an unrelenting power structure. The long reels of red tape involved in something as minor yet crucial as pinpointing the appropriate department to address with each specific concern presented overwhelming obstacles. Moreover, most residents had pressing needs for employment, housing, and mere survival in the immediate sense. Many of the committee's demands for further material compensation, report Clairmont and Magill, were neither accepted nor rejected, but merely put off until they faded away with the bulk of the tenuous governmental commitments.

While the later 1960s and the 1970s saw heightened black activism in Nova Scotia generally, the new radical politics came too late either to save Africville or to effectively rally on its behalf for better housing or compensation. Rather, the outcome of the destruction served as a catalyst for organizing and for a more widespread awareness that other black communities might be vulnerable to similar plans. At the time of Africville's existence and that of its destruction, many whites and blacks alike subscribed to the liberal rhetoric of integration. For instance, some Africville residents noted that other Halifax blacks were unsupportive of their cause,[83] and the black activists on the Human Rights Advisory Committee had supported the goal of integration. The rise of militancy seems to have occurred, understandably, at the tail end of dislocation, when the city's broken promises were becoming more apparent and as tenets of broader anti-racist movements, such as Black Power in the United States, reached a relatively isolated population. Given the deceptive and chaotic way in which the city demolished Africville, it is not surprising that hindsight might offer a clearer view of an incomprehensible program of eradication masquerading as rescue.

The Destruction of Africville Interpreted

A Geography of Racism

When the destruction of Africville is examined as part of a larger historical context in which the spatial management of Nova Scotia's black population is the dominant trope, the view that white officials were concerned with improving the conditions of blacks and wished to integrate them into white society becomes more difficult to support.

Africville was born from a legacy of slavery and segregation. From the outset of black residency in Nova Scotia, those who were not slaves were allotted infertile land on the outskirts of white towns. These were the areas not marked on maps, and where the pavement ended; they were 'approaches' to the legitimate spaces of towns and cities; they were expendable until required by whites. These were the people to whom governments neglected to grant land title, keeping them stagnant, their property illegitimate, tenuous. Violence and hostility were the common responses to blacks' presence among whites, particularly those from the struggling working classes, who saw them as competition for scarce jobs and resources. To the middle and wealthier classes, blacks were sources of cheap labour, signifying and abiding by the domestic and urban spatial boundaries that distinguished servant from master.

Africville, established in the hopes of reduced isolation and improved access to resources, soon faced the stigma of the racial slum. Polluted with industries and waste products, it became the 'residual city,' the 'place apart,' the repository composed of the delineation between pure and undefiled white space and contaminated blackness.

Authorities who observed and spoke of Africville narrated abhorrent circumstances, in which the city's role was obscured or forgotten. They portrayed only what was visible to the eye – filth, the slum, desolation, 'scavenging.' These conditions made the necessary removal axiomatic to most Haligonians. Reports of 'degenerate' lifestyles in Africville functioned to portray residents as helpless and infantile, in need of others to make decisions on their behalf, to rescue their community through its excision.

As David Goldberg has suggested, the spatial technologies for containing racial difference evolve over time. The 1960s saw a drastic increase in the diagnoses of social pathology among poor and racialized populations by white experts. This did not signify a humanitarian shift on the part of these experts, but rather, a social and moral panic that conditions in neglected and abused slum areas had grown out of control and threatened to impede the development of healthy cities. As Stallybrass and White have theorized, the slums of urban areas had long been viewed as contaminating agents, capable of spilling their crime and immorality upon the upper classes. The solution involved figuring out the most effective manner of containing the disorder, and reforming it where possible. Goldberg writes:

> Whether the bodies of the racialized Other were to be killed or colonized, slaughtered or saved, expunged or exploited, they had to be prevented at all costs from polluting the body politic or sullying civil(ized) society. Impurity, dirt, disease, and pollution ... are expressed by way of transgressing classificatory categories, as also are danger and the breakdown of order. Threatening to transgress or pollute established social order necessitates their reinvention, first by conceptualizing order anew and then by reproducing spatial confinement and separation in the renewed terms.[84]

This renewal saw the onset of project administration as a means of containing social deviance, creating an appearance of integration by placing these new residences in the city, often in the centre of white neighbourhoods, making possible the closer observation of their residents' activities.

There is little indication that the ideological bent of these programs involved significant moves toward equality. As can be seen in the 'relocation' era, no long-term plans were in place for employment programs, educational opportunities, retraining, or independent housing initiatives. Decision makers made little attempt to understand residents' positions, or to facilitate their future independence.

Africville's designation as a space outside society was cemented in the process of negotiation and settlement. Throughout the process of dislocation, Africville people were kept at a spatial distance consistent with their historical treatment. The boundaries between the city proper and Africville were traversed by whites only for the purposes of study, or to convince the people of their one option to move after the decision had been largely finalized at city hall. Decision making itself occurred in official white spaces, and residents were occasionally invited in when the purpose suited city officials. Those who represented their interests also maintained their distance; over 80 per cent of residents later reported that they had had no contact whatsoever with the Halifax Human Rights Advisory Committee (HHRAC), including its black members. Most community members were never aware that people were purporting to fight for them, or of what in particular they were asking on Africville's behalf.[85]

Advisory committee members admittedly knew little about Africville, and their contact with its residents was limited mainly to the few people working with them as activists. Members mentioned the lack of services and resources in the community, but knew little of day-to-day life. One white man recalled having been to Africville only a few times, 'usually at night,' while another had only occasionally 'driven through.' One man, when asked if he knew people from Africville, recalled having hired a maid from Africville who had come to work badly beaten.[86] Another member reported, speculatively:

I think there was a lot of escape there, through heavy drinking ... I heard reports about policemen who were unwilling to go into Africville unless there were two or three of them ... Physical violence, I understand, took place. Bitter rivalries between certain individuals apparently developed through the years ... Just imagine not having running water. Imagine being so much cut off.[87]

Committee members' observations are frequently underscored by rumour, pity, and dominant stereotypes. Their perceptions and experiences are organized around spatial divisions which encode the race and class divide; they directly reflect and reinforce the racial discourses operative in this time.

When asked their reasons for wanting to help, whites spoke of outrage at the appalling conditions in the community, and a belief in the need to provide equal opportunities for all people to reach their potential. Black members, several of whom were motivated by concern for their racial group and a high degree of political consciousness,[88] more explicitly criticized the city and praised Africville's community spirit. Still, all non-Africville members knew little of the community's residents, saw their futures as inevitably doomed to dislocation, and agreed with desegregation. While they were undoubtedly more sympathetic than the city and explored more options for Africville, they occupied a representational position that was largely imposed on Africville, and they saw forced integration as the only solution.

The ground upon which decisions were made was never neutral. For instance, the summoning of Pa Carvery to city hall positioned one black man against a committee of whites, in their space, on their terms. What does it mean to be summoned to cross the physical and metaphorical boundary between white and black space when one is clearly the player without power? What does it mean in an urban space known for verbal, physical, and legal racist assaults, a space in which one might not be served in a restaurant or leased an apartment? When an act such as this is situated in history, in contemporary society, and in space, it means much more than an unacceptable business proposal between equal parties.

The process of dislocation was never designed to facilitate participation by Africville residents. While the city justified this exclusion through a guise of respect for privacy, they had ravaged Africville land, invaded Africville lives, and defined for the people what privacy, respect, and community itself must mean. Even the alleged concern for racial equality was a discussion in which blacks, in this instance, had little voice. Segregation, in the white perspective, was bound up in the cultural pathology of black community, and responsible for a destructive cohesiveness that kept the people in their impoverished state.

Desegregation, presented as a positive liberal aim, actually camouflaged the common rhetoric of black degeneracy, with its abolition contingent upon white example and rescue.

Paternalistic disdain for Africville was justified through the evidence of its landscape. In a cyclic manner, the community was deprived of resources, forced to cope with less, and then blamed for the way it survived. Poor conditions framed Africville as a bad investment for the city, thus things were never to improve. Morality became intricately tied to the apparent social disorder of the space. Lower settlements based on the alleged immoral character of particular residents are a good example of this; in depriving some of better compensation, the city again placed responsibility for the state of people's lives squarely on their own heads. Supported by the HHRAC, who admittedly knew almost nothing of Africville, the city obscured its own central role in creating conditions in which the people suffered, only to further deprive them based on the situation they were in. Through moral judgment, spatial distance, exclusion from the decision-making process, intimidation, and manipulative portrayals of character, dominant actors maintained Africville as a site of the 'internal Other'[89] to be feared, controlled, and ultimately destroyed.

Africville residents found organization for compensation and other community goals increasingly difficult following their forced move. While a number moved to Uniacke Square, others were dispersed throughout the province, and the trials of day-to-day survival, the adjustment to a new environment, and the fractious stresses imposed on community relations by the city's divisive relocation settlements, had taken their toll. Their marginal community was recolonized in a few different sites and with newly imposed controls. Goldberg writes:

> As the social margins are (re)colonized or cut loose, the peripheral is symbolically wiped away. With no place to gather and dislocated from any sense of community, it becomes that much more difficult for dispossessed individuals to offer resistance both to their material displacement and to the rationalizing characterizations that accompany the dislocation.[90]

The new projects into which many residents were placed enabled the imposition of stricter standards with regard to family composition, order of households, individual expression,[91] and community cohesion. Much poverty continued or worsened, and these projects quickly developed an enduring racial stigma of their own, suggesting support for the view that social problems move with the poor and racialized, rather than with the city's regulatory policy.

Contested Reason(s)

> Patterns of living developed over the years can't be broken down overnight. This is an economic, psychological, educational integration into the community as a whole, which necessarily takes time and cooperation between City Council, the established community and Africville residents.[92]

> When the community is broken up, some of the better elements in the community may be influenced by their neighbours to improve their conditions.[93]

These statements encompass a number of official explanations offered for the destruction of Africville. They suggest that integration will bring positive results as blacks are influenced by the civilized society of whites. The former suggests the relocation program is a contractual agreement among all parties, who are working together. The latter makes moral distinctions between 'better elements' and a largely hopeless population. It upholds the belief that whites offer the best solution as well as the best alternative social environments, and squarely supports 'social pathology' theories that blame community cohesion for the continued strife in racialized areas: culture, as a stand-in for race, creates its own flawed conditions, and only through its interruption and dispersal can individuals begin to imagine corrective measures.

At another level, there is writing on the destruction of Africville that is critical of the process. Various authors aim to make sense of what happened, to discern the reasons behind the city's policy and to judge its success or failure based on the outcome. The *Relocation Report* by Clairmont and Magill addresses these concerns, and various theses, articles, or reports using other media make their own evaluations. Some work aims to explore aspects of the community's life that have been largely neglected in historical accounts; for example, Susan Precious has studied the roles and contributions of Africville women. Both her research and that of Sheridan Hay broaches relations among black and white women, and both authors point to the systemic and ongoing nature of racism. Accounts of the story by black writers often focus on the life of the community, well-known people who lived there, or the political resistance that has stemmed from the Africville experience. Commemoration, recovery of missing stories and the preservation of history, community spirit and all it stands for are the key themes in many works about Africville's life and destruction.

In this section, I do not aim to replicate commemorative efforts or to appropriate the political struggle catalyzed by Africville's history. I suggest, however, that there is space, and a need, for something else. There are surprisingly few critical accounts of the Africville destruction that explicitly name racism. When it is acknowledged, rarely is it tied directly to the essence of dominant white actions and intentions in the removal of the community. Here, I critique some common ways of reading Africville's destruction, with a view to illuminating a different analysis.

The fact of racism as a primary organizing principle of social relations in Nova Scotia is often forgotten or obscured in dominant white interpretations of Africville's story. Although it is commonly acknowledged as part of a broader 'context,' or one of many problems *in* society, there can be a failure to connect it at the root of the dislocation decision, as fundamental to the structure of the process. The relocation decision was a microcosm of the way in which society functions as a whole; it embodies the larger set of technologies by which whites carry out the spatial regulation of blacks. More often, however, racism is seen only as a complicating factor that contributes to the problems of Africville people and the way they were viewed by the white media and the general public. Further, when acknowledgments are made that racism was present in society, and even that the city of Halifax treated Africville 'badly,' racial discourses are not explored. This makes it difficult to see how the destruction was intricately tied to existing and persisting notions of racial difference.

Racism has been taken up in white accounts of Africville as, variably, a set of individual beliefs, as whites simply believing themselves to be 'superior' to blacks, or as something which occurred 'in history.' When defined as an attitude problem, it can be confined to certain individuals, and seen as exceptional or errant. Bernard MacDougall, for instance, discusses segregation as a result of individual prejudices in some neighbourhoods.[94] As a complicating issue in what happened to the black population, racism remains a legacy of the past, not something that continues to be reproduced in different terms. When it is seen as an ongoing struggle, it is sometimes characterized as a problem in 'race relations,' implying that different groups simply have trouble getting along. One thesis identifies the 'unpleasantness' of this conflict.[95] Such 'equalizing' narratives sidestep the discomfort of naming who is enacting dominance. The problem of racism can be seen as simply an entity existing 'out there'; it is effectively disconnected from the process of destruction in important ways.

For one, racism is seen as responsible for the historical oppression of blacks, which has resulted in their current poor economic conditions. These economic conditions, in turn, become the prime source of their troubles in the present. It is these current problems that city officials must effectively treat. Further, racism is disconnected from any actors in the relocation decision. Even when sharply criticized for the 'mistakes' they made, officials and planners are seen to be dealing with the problems created by historical oppression; they are not enacting dominance themselves but, quite the opposite, are in the process of correcting it.

Perhaps most blatantly, the city utilized specific mechanisms for controlling against accusations of racism, attempting to completely reverse such interpretations. They attributed the long existence of Africville to the special treatment it had received based on the race of its inhabitants, claiming it would have been demolished much sooner had the residents not been black. The city also emphasized its history of leniency in allowing deviant activity, such as drinking and parties, to proceed, and allowing scavenging on the dump against municipal ordinance. Such leniency was extended during the relocation era, as the city constantly reiterated its concern in doing more than was legally necessary, going beyond the requirements of compensation. This was backed up in the local paper, which frequently cited the municipality's fairness and generosity. It is exemplified in one letter stating, 'the people of Africville seem to think their part of Halifax has been singled out ... for special treatment. This is true only insofar as the Board, on humanitarian grounds, has recommended that the full weight of the law "be tempered with understanding and natural justice."'[96] When Albert Rose visited Africville, he later told Clairmont, he warned the mayor that the relocation plan risked being viewed as 'negro removal' and specified ways to avoid this label. For instance, the city hoped that the addition of black officials on committees would forestall the accusation.

The termination of Africville is frequently seen not only as a product of a history contributing to the present, but to a somewhat unintelligible 'system' that failed to function properly. For instance, Clairmont and Magill, while they certainly acknowledge the reality of racism in society, stress the fault of 'bureaucracy' and its confusing and disorganized nature, in failing to produce better results. They state that blaming individuals would amount merely to unhelpful 'scapegoating,'[97] since problems lie in the overall structure of the plan. While I agree that no single individual can be blamed, and there were indeed numerous examples of structural and organizational incompetence, I question the assumption that it is fruitless to criticize individual actions. Bureaucracies are made up of individuals, responsibilities exist on every level, and at some point, individuals must be held accountable for their roles. Otherwise, bureaucracy and 'the system' become amorphous, intangible structures that can simply override human agency. Rather than a critical interrogation of how the system might be changed from within, we are allowed detachment from a larger depersonalized entity, thus from responsibility. Moreover, we miss the ways in which bureaucracies themselves are instrumental in maintaining relations of power.

A thesis by Christopher Riou, too, asserts that the dislocation was not a conscious racist decision among whites, but had to do with a long history of neglect and 'ignorance.' Again, a notion of the relocation as a corrective approach to a historical problem is upheld, while it is too easy to forget that history is created and written by human beings. This also implies a clear cut-off point between past and present. In attributing Africville's end to the commonplaceness of urban renewal at the time, we can fail to see how urban renewal is structured epistemologically by racial discourses similar to those that structured colonialism and that continue to structure spatial management.

Riou's thesis is centrally concerned with the notion of 'progress' in determining Africville's end. He conducts a detailed and insightful critique of one newspaper's reporting on the process of demolition, concluding that the paper was instrumental in upholding the city's dominant beliefs and plans. As Riou notes, mainly 'official' voices were quoted, while Africville residents' views were almost completely absent. Riou argues that respectable voices were those who were able to define and implement 'progressive' policies, whether the speakers were black or white. While I agree, the work does not attend to how whites in respectable positions viewed *blackness itself* to be incompatible with progress and respectability. Historical racism is posited as a contributing factor in the poor life-conditions of blacks in the present, but the fact that the black community remains outside notions of progress in contemporary society is attributed to these conditions, not to their blackness; race remains one step removed. To see how these notions interlock, it is essential to examine racial discourse. Specific narratives about the degeneracy of blackness and black community fuelled white justifications for the spatial subjugation of the marginalized group. Racism and the drive for progress do not simply exist, each separately, at the same time. Rather, race structures how progress can be conceptualized. Similarly, Riou and others locate racism in the 'exclusion' of blacks from public life. While this is part of the equation, white citizens are not simply engaging in the contemporary reconstruction of white spaces and leaving blacks 'behind.' Blackness is necessary to notions of progress, providing a backdrop against which the respectable and progressive white self can be understood as legitimately dominant. Riou's work, while rightly critical of how the newsmedia privileges certain voices, presents an analysis of respectability that is not raced.[98]

Africville is often portrayed as having been 'stuck in time.' Susan Dexter's article in *Maclean's* is pointedly titled 'The Black Ghetto that Fears Integration,' suggesting that the community is clinging to its past, irrationally intimidated by modern living. This obscures the fact that residents had long been petitioning for modern services, were eager to grow as a community, and had already accepted many changes over the years. 'Fears' of integration, on the other hand, were rational considering the enduringly hostile climate of Halifax; however, these fears were clearly not the reason for any delays in the demolition process since the city did not consider residents' views in the first place. How did the ongoing struggle for modern services and building permits for the upkeep of homes signify a desire to cling to outmoded lifestyles? Again, the community was forced into stagnation and then labelled with a fear of the development process that was constructed without its involvement. Reporters commonly suggest a dichotomy between Africville's traditional nature and the city's modernizing impulse. This misrepresents Africville residents' expressed desires and suggests that their community life was seen to be antiquated, when in fact it had been deeply pathologized.

Planners, government workers, researchers, and others frequently reiterated that the time had come when 'something needed to be done' about Africville.[99] However, the white community overlooked that residents were more than aware of this, and had been proposing solutions and attempting positive steps for decades. The reality, then, was less that the time had come, than that whites had finally conceded what Africville had known all along.

The *Relocation Report* acknowledges the city's paternal attitude, which is exemplified in officials' responses to questions about their intent. Clairmont and Magill openly asked officials, 'why did the City relocate Africville?' Their answers centred on the improvement of living conditions and desegregation, echoing the *Mail Star*'s declaration that 'social necessity and sound financial reasoning require integration.'[100] The mayor confirmed that industrial development was not a concern, stating that, had that been the case, Africville would still exist. Officials also spoke of the uncontrolled nature of Africville's growing problems, frequently stating that people could no longer be 'permitted' to live this way.[101] The report conveys officials' deep sense of moral outrage that things had been allowed to spiral out of control. This fact is attributed to a shameful neglect that, while true, serves to emphasize the inaction, rather than the action of the city in making Africville as it was. Attributing conditions to the city's 'ignorance' bolsters the view that Africville slowly disintegrated on its own due to its isolation from the city, which knew little about the consequences. It ignores the conscious actions of placing the dump, for instance, appropriating land for rail lines, building factories and incinerators, and refusing services.

A prevailing theory among white commentators suggests that the city of Halifax, while perhaps insensitive or naive, desired the integration of the black community into white society, along with the improved quality of life and opportunity for blacks. That is, the underlying motive is seen to be improvement, the promise of integration upheld as the central impetus. Based on the evidence I have explored here, and the proliferation of racial discourses about Africville and the black community generally, it seems clear that integration was not a key interest in the city's move to demolish Africville, regardless of what was said. The rhetoric of integration, rather, is an appropriation of black political terms to obscure a project of white regulation and containment of black people. While this contention will not be new to most blacks affected by Africville's history, it is disturbing to the liberal notion that community demolition was a product of its time or a result of mistakes in the past.

The *Relocation Report* and a resulting thesis by Dennis Magill[102] present various potentially positive factors, which seem to indicate a careful, detailed planning approach. The authors cite the advice of Rose, a 'nationally renowned welfare expert,' the many discussions about the problems in Africville, and the formation of the human rights committee of black and white professionals. They note that city officials were required to clearly articulate their plans, and that many layers of debate ensued before any action could be approved. They also mention the availability of assistance funds, which were to cut down on the bureaucratic problems of obtaining emergency money for residents. The plan included employment and educational programs, and was purportedly geared toward the improvement of life opportunities for blacks.

In the report, the official liberal welfare rhetoric of integration and organized social change is accepted as the dominant concern of officials and activists involved. All these factors are seen to illustrate the benevolent objectives behind the program. While the authors do conclude that the program was largely unsuccessful, the foundational assumption of positive intent is not disrupted.[103] Rather, they identify general bureaucratic issues that are not linked to specific persons. For example: 'the relocatees had to negotiate settlements with a City agency that had neither the official mandate nor the resources necessary to undertake a broad program of planned social change.'[104] This common passive tone leaves the impression that the lack of mandate and resources are at fault, much like the above 'bureaucracy' or 'system.' Again, an exploration of racial discourse would suffuse these abstract phenomena with a deeper sense of *how* the system operates, challenging one to consider, for instance, how officials and planners looked upon, studied, and spoke about Africville, and how this shaped policy.

The *Relocation Report* demonstrates more than any other source the explicit actions of individual people and the views and concerns of all involved. Without a critical race analysis, however, we are left unable to name the racism present. In the foreword to a recent edition of their book, Clairmont and Magill reflect that their views have changed over the years, and that they no longer agree with the rhetoric of relocation itself. However, they still maintain the altruistic forethought of the city. Similarly, MacDougall, in his study of the program's results, addresses the city's reasoning at face value. His thinking is steeped in a belief in the benefits of urban renewal programs and does not question the structure of the plan itself. Aiming, primarily, to consider the 'human' side of relocation, the author cites family breakdown as the dominant problem, leaving any failures in the program largely upon the heads of residents, whose chaotic lifestyle made their adaptation impossible. The challenges he notes are those faced by authorities in convincing Africville residents to cooperate in their plans. This sentiment is echoed in news reports that cite, for instance, the many 'setbacks and disappointments' that authorities faced during the dislocation.[105] Clearly, observers made various moral judgments as to how well residents were seen to cope with their new surroundings. Another news article states that many families had 'satisfied authorities that they are really trying to adapt to a new life.'[106]

Like Clairmont and Magill, MacDougall defends the process as having been contemplated carefully over a long period of time. He, however, is less sympathetic to residents' concerns, stating that they had been willing only to hear information that would prevent relocation, and that they expressed 'widespread hostility and suspicion.'

MacDougall portrays the city as compassionate and patient, having been willing to negotiate and consult with residents. Their investment in legal aid and the many meetings they held are seen as evidence of their commitment to positive change. He frequently notes the great length of the planning process, and is selective in reporting the views of residents who did not mind moving, and a few people who spoke ill of Africville. MacDougall evaluates the success of the relocation in terms of how well authorities communicated their plans to residents, and how well residents were able to understand information about what would happen. Another factor was simply the act of being able to move people in this large-scale manner. Since Africville had been deemed a population of 'low geographic mobility,' the city's capability in moving them at all is positioned as a significant accomplishment.

MacDougall's only point of contention is that the city could have been more successful in gaining the trust of the people. Thus the aim is to improve upon relocation models so that future projects will result in fewer complaints. His solution is that, in future, residents should be educated about relocation by 'their own kind of people'[107] who have themselves learned to deal successfully with relocation.

Like other studies, MacDougall's work and the approach in the *Relocation Report* do not problematize the methodological tensions when relatively privileged, white researchers enter a poor, black community. This critical gap allows a sense that all involved have simply reported their 'true feelings,' and the profound power differentials are unacknowledged. For instance, might people in black communities have shaped their answers to protect privacy, to avoid conflict with whites, or to appear more respectable? Further, the residents had been studied to no end and were exhausted by whites who interrogated them but whose work never resulted in benefits, and sometimes caused harm. In the period immediately following relocation, it is doubtful that residents were enthusiastic about yet another study, particularly when they could expect no beneficial follow-up.

Why were so many people shocked at the lack of follow-up to Africville's removal? Given the historical context, the widespread desire to be rid of the problem, the racial discourses structuring the decision, and the manner in which the move was carried out, I would argue, this surprise is quite unfounded. However, I too was initially shocked. Even aside from my abhorrence of the community's destruction, I could not believe the overwhelming mess of disorganization and bad planning. After more reflection, I realized my own reaction was inconsistent with my analysis: It was never built into the structure of the program that the move should be followed-up. It was never part of the plan that residents' lives should be greatly improved. These empty promises never attended to specificities, and never resulted in concrete planning or consultation. Looking more closely at what was said during meetings and in letters, it is apparent how city officials' discourse becomes general and vague when residents ask about particular plans. Meetings in Africville were scheduled after decisions had been made. No one recorded promises, and, newspaper articles portrayed these promises as misguided notions made up by bitter Africville people. The development officer's mandate was to 'get the thing cleaned up' without controversy.

An analysis of how the city might begin to attack the problems of Africville at the systemic level, and a commitment to policies based on residents' own volition would have been completely incongruous with the project of removal. What occurred was more or less exactly what was intended: Africville was bulldozed, most blacks were contained within 'black areas' in public housing projects, city officials rid themselves of the embarrassment of the segregated slum, and washed their hands of their 'racial problem.' The plan was not disorganized; it was just organized enough.

Conclusion

It is easy for white people to tell a story of Africville without speaking the word race. Such stories are told often. They begin, often, in the slum, a site of misfortune. Those who live there have had difficult lives due to history. They have few resources, little income, and barely enough education to comprehend their circumstances. They survive by banding together in shared deprivation, constructing shacks and scavenging off the larger community's giant waste pile (which happens to sit at their front door). Over years, the larger society has grown, evolved, and left them behind. It is now time to help them catch up. Experts and scholars have studied society long enough to know that segregation and poverty can be corrected with intervention, and that the poor, being difficult to mobilize and having little knowledge of the real world, require a firm hand from those who have come to understand their lives. City officials who execute slum clearance programs are acting on the advice of experts, who they have employed. Rarely is the clearance their own idea, although they often agree with its necessity, as any reasonable citizen would. When these programs fail, or are unsatisfactory to those who are removed from their homes, this is yet another unfortunate fact of life. It is possible, of course, that officials acted with insufficient knowledge of the community; they can make decisions based only on the information provided to them by those who perform the research. The researchers simply observe and report the real conditions they encounter when they enter the slum. The information they unearth and circulate is all that is available. Any reasonable person also knows that the solution proposed and carried out was the only thing to do.

Still, the dislocated poor are enraged. They request explanations but are never satisfied with those offered. They continue to demand justice, not understanding that compensation has already been paid. They have been rescued from themselves, from history, brought not only to safety, but to respectable surroundings, which may even rub off on them. However, the more this is explained to them, the more confused they become. Meetings have been held, city officials have listened and waited patiently through various tantrums, and still they are accused of insensitivity. Not only this, but they are still asked to account for those elusive 'historical circumstances.' As more and more generosity is shown, the more angry the residents grow. It is almost as if they are incapable of understanding reason, almost as if they are simply different from us after all. In fact, there is a risk that they may become violent; the city may be forced to take precautions, and so on ...

As late as 1970, when it had become apparent to many Haligonians that the dislocation had caused irreparable harm to Africville residents, *Time* magazine declared, 'The bulldozing of Africville exemplifies a determined, if belated, effort by the municipal and provincial government, to right an historical injustice.'[108] This quite succinctly embodies the official white story. It teaches the public that the destruction of a black community against its will was done precisely for the good of all black people. It is about integration, the equalizing of opportunities, and the creation of a comprehensive community in which difference does not matter. These are qualities anyone, save the anomalous overt bigot, would embrace. Further, the city and province, in this project, have acted not to correct any mistakes of their own, but to address those of the past, for which they are not even responsible. Perhaps they left it a little late, but there is still time – history, once finished, isn't going anywhere.

The dominant, raceless story includes unspecified notions of difference, but it is difference without hierarchies. It is not a story in which some groups are disempowered and others privileged. The dominant white story is one in which people have choices, a story out of space and time. It is a story about reason, about unavoidable disasters and about helplessness. Then it is a white story about unfounded blame, about resentment and rage, about the irrational acting out of children. This story *does* explain why accountability is impossible, how misfortune can strike where well-meaning subjects have merely tried to help. It is a story in which we acknowledge both sides of the argument, but only one makes sense.

The process of demolishing Africville was a program planned by whites to shift the strategies used to contain a small black community. It was bolstered by racist discourses, yet camouflaged in the promise of racial integration. It attempted to save face for the city by hiding its racial problem, yet made no moves toward systemic change. Instead, the discursive focus on slum clearance masked the city's crucial role in creating the impoverished conditions in question, and relied on racial narratives in preserving a conflation of black community itself with moral and social degeneracy.

Forced dislocation is enabled through a variety of techniques: a fundamental racism that sets a group apart physically and metaphorically from the dominant community; the manufacture, through both neglect and strategic planning, of a space against which progress, identity, entitlement, purity, and civility can be measured; a program of displacement supported by the majority of citizens, based on these factors; and the appearance of a humanitarian motive. It is furthered by built-in controls for deflecting critique or accusations of race discrimination, and the reliance on expert, respectable opinion. With these factors firmly in place, it is astonishing how easily the racism and negligence behind a particular endeavour can be masked, and transposed into a story of empathy and benevolence.

The deficient planning and apparent incompetence of officials in the Africville program were not mistakes; they were part and parcel of a conscious wish for Africville to simply fade away, for the *visibility* of segregation and poverty to subside. Given the ideological climate and history, and the way in which plans were carried out, there is no reasonable basis from which to accept that the problems following relocation were unintended or, at the very least, could not have been foreseen. There is every reason to suggest that a program of white displacement of black people, which maintained their spatial regulation and social disenfranchisement, was the logical continuation of race domination. The liberal rhetoric of integration and renewal, never realized, was in fact a discourse and a practice of erasure from sight and site.

5 Reconciling Africville:
The Politics of Dreaming and Forgetting

The enlightened notion that one can learn from history has been so violently disproved both at the social and the political levels as well as in its experiential dimension that the very legitimacy of the historical enterprise is shaken.

Andreas Huyssen[1]

Africville's story does not dissolve in the failed promises of 1968 or fade with a docile black population. Rather, a united and politicized black community has emerged over the last several decades as the force behind commemorative and compensatory efforts. Africville has come to stand for community, resistance, and survival, and it has been the subject of many artistic endeavours. With such widespread dialogue and remembrance, how have racial discourse and the story of Africville changed among the dominant white population? How has the city responded to ongoing challenges, and how have whites generally chosen to remember or forget? While the black community necessarily and vocally tells its own story, there is, I argue here, a continuing story of race and regulation to be told. This is a story of the dominant group's grappling – or disengaging – with the impact of racism and of Africville on the past and present; it has received little or no critical attention among white or black writers. While forms of discussion around and about Africville may have shifted, much has remained the same. Material gains for former residents have increased little, and white accountability for the past and present has yet to be claimed. The city continues to regulate the physical space of Africville. This has significant implications for the story of dislocation that is told and heard.

How dominant subjects engage with and learn from the stories of subjugated groups is deeply influenced by narratives of innocence that
operate through the containment of 'mistakes' in the past and the suppression of stories of domination.

Like the liberal good intentions of the relocation era, attention to commemorative initiatives does not lead seamlessly to material progress for
the dominated group, nor to the rethinking of hierarchical relations
among the dominant. On the contrary, the reconstruction of memory
occurs through complex negotiations over social spaces, pedagogical
positions, ideological backgrounds, and material resources. It is never
divorced from the historical relations among dominant and subjugated
groups that originally underpinned the events being remembered.
Introducing his analysis of postwar Germany's struggle over newly
uncovered sites of memory for Jews, Henri Lustiger-Thaler writes:

> One group's need to remember is often grist for another's desire to forget.
> It is not surprising that acts of public commemoration have as much stra-
> tegically inscribed within them as they have excluded. Memory and for-
> getting are hence part of an embedded historical discourse that evokes as
> it simultaneously erases, inevitably unfolding on many different social
> registers and in different 'memory encounters' between groups, as they
> attempt to articulate their sense of (dis)location within the present.[2]

Considerations of such 'memory encounters' now constitute a growing field of inquiry about how stories of violence are to be written and
retold, and by whom. The complexities of the use and reclamation of
social space are embedded in these confrontations. For example, Lisa
Yoneyama has studied efforts at urban renewal in modern-day
Hiroshima that are entangled in the city's desired presentation of its
history and national narrative. Through attempts to decentre memory
of the war and to downplay the nearly axiomatic cognitive conflation
of the city with the atom bomb, Yoneyama argues, Hiroshima has
engaged in a project of reforming the cityscape to carve out 'new
knowledge and consciousness, as well as amnesia, about history and
society.'[3] While occupying very different contexts from each other and
from Halifax, the examples of Hiroshima and Germany assert that the
regulation and reconstruction of space are inextricably linked to how
memory and forgetting can occur. As Jennifer Schirmer shows in her
discussion of women's peace movements, space figures centrally in the
politics of protest and resistance as well. She writes, '[Just as] ideology

is resisted through counter-ideological practices so, too, is the state's control of public space resisted by forms of spatialized disobedience, primarily through the use of speech and the body.'[4]

In Halifax, blacks and whites encounter the memory of Africville differently as they witness the transformation of its former site, the establishment of a park and a monument to the black community in its stead on the site, and city responses to the continued 'spatialized disobedience' of Africville's bodies and voices. The black community is successfully spreading its story and this is not my task. My task is to examine how and why we as whites cannot hear the story as one connected to our own lives. While public symbols of acknowledgment and commemoration now exist, they are limited in their ability to instil a sense of collective memorial space for a variety of reasons. These reasons are rooted in the historical racial narratives and spatial arrangements that constitute the Other *as Other,* and the dominant group as 'us,' and as innocent. We, as dominant group members, must understand how we come to the lessons of memory by a very different route from those retelling their history. We must recognize that receiving new information is insufficient when it fails to deepen our grasp of complex power relations and our own positions within them.

In the first part of this chapter, I discuss some central forms and themes of black commemoration of Africville. Analysis of black literature and other art forms is not the focus of this work, however, it is important to understand the contemporary place Africville holds in a community still fighting to survive. Such a story must be the central template upon which white outsiders consider our responses and responsibilities in remembering. Further, I want to establish outright a sense of the black voices shaping dialogue about Africville today, lest my focus on white discourse risk obliterating the agency of these activists or suggesting only their victimization.

The balance of the chapter examines responses from white community officials to ongoing critique and demands for compensation from former Africville residents. For this, I take two complementary paths. The first explores dominant narratives that operate to reconstitute the past and to deflect criticism. The second examines city actions taken in attempt to define the official history of Africville, including the establishment of Seaview Park as a public recreational site, and various disputes over its use and preservation. In this analysis I also consider how the media have employed dominant racial narratives in conveying the events. While there is significant overlap, in the second section I aim to establish ongoing racial discourses, and in the third the focus is more explicitly on the central acts these discourses have accompanied or enabled. I conclude with consideration of the monument to Africville in Seaview Park, as both an actual and metaphoric tool that shapes how memory is articulated.

Once again, my use of 'we' and 'our' is strategic, not unconscious. I do address white readers specifically, insofar as the themes presented here constitute a particular challenge to them. I acknowledge my own struggle with this challenge as well. This does not intend to exclude non-white readers, only to acknowledge that the kind of analytic and reflexive work to be undertaken does not apply to them in the same way, and that I do not purport to know what work is needed within their communities. However, a consideration of how whites receive and respond to Africville's story is, possibly, useful to any reader, and may be a contribution to strategies of resistance for black activists.

I am also cognizant that the categories of white and black are never so clearly divided. It can hardly be assumed that all blacks feel similarly about Africville, or that whites are never critical. Some efforts at justice and commemoration have been collaborative across communities. Some Africville residents felt abandoned by blacks in other parts of the province who didn't rally to help them at the time of relocation. I am, however, speaking of general delineations that remain strong. This may be difficult to take for granted if one is unfamiliar with Halifax or smaller areas in Nova Scotia, which are still often visibly segregated. The tone of racism in these areas is particular, and the story of Africville has to be regarded in its social and historical context. In this light, I proceed with some generalizations, while keeping in mind a space in which white and black, and the boundaries between them, matter a great deal.

A Keystone of Community

I am Africville
says a woman, child, man at the homestead site.
This park is green; but
Black, so Black with community.
I talk Africville
to you
and to you
until it is both you and me

till it stands and lives again
till you face and see and stand
on its life and its forever
Black past.   Maxine Tynes, 'Africville'[5]

While city views were always contested, it has become more common to read black critique, to hear commemorative words, and to witness organized resistance to racist acts of the past and present. A rich body of literature, artwork, and music, dubbed by writer George Elliott Clarke the 'Africadian Cultural Renaissance,' now depicts the contemporary meaning of Africville as a site of protest, a point of black pride, and a lesson for all. This stanza, from a poem by Maxine Tynes, encompasses what many Africadian writers have called the 'spirit' of Africville. They refer to the power of shared history in bringing people together, enriching their common struggles. Africville has come to be a rallying cry for the black community, a symbol of what can happen if they are not vigilant and organized in their own interests. Tynes's work asserts that Africville now matters most as history to be passed on and as a symbol of black unity and resistance. Charles Saunders, too, writes, 'Africville is not a memory frozen in the amber of history. It's continuing to grow, to evolve, just as it did from the 1840s to the 1960s. Once it was a place. Now it's a spirit, an icon, a metaphor, a home.'[6]

Opened in 1989, an exhibition at Mount Saint Vincent University in Halifax reflected these values, telling the stories of former residents and depicting the daily life of the community through photos, artifacts, audio-visual aids, and written documentation. This exhibit was the result of collaborative efforts among black Africville Genealogical Society members and both black and white researchers and artists. Now housed in the Black Cultural Centre of Nova Scotia, it is a rich portrayal of memory in the form of a 'walk' through the community. Such narrative brings a heightened sense of the concreteness of Africville's life, igniting a stronger realization that something very much alive and worthwhile has been lost. Pictures present evidence in a way oral claims alone cannot, and the stories are told in text in an accompanying catalogue. Stories of Africville have also been set to music by jazz artist Joe Sealy,[7] interpreted in a radio performance by local artist David Wood,[8] and published in a book that includes analytic work.[9]

Shortly after the exhibition, a National Film Board documentary was produced, entitled *Remember Africville*.[10] In this film, the way of life in the community is again depicted through stories from older residents, live footage, and photography. It also covers interviews with residents about their forced removal from their community, and follows a contemporary conference between black community members and city council, in which residents interrogate the city as to its actions during the destruction of Africville. Here, residents suggest their community was an experiment in social design and they the guinea pigs. They attest to the great emotional loss and physical fear surrounding relocation. A former mayor of Halifax responds with rhetoric strikingly similar to that used in the 1960s. Reading directly from a transcript, he tells residents that the city merely followed the advice of experts in the field of urban renewal, naming Albert Rose and others, in line with common values of the time. He assures them that Africville would be treated differently today; if the situation were to arise again, their views would be sought firsthand.

Black interviewees in the film assert the value of Africville as a home and community; they express their anger at city neglect and appear frustrated at the remaining absence of a thorough explanation. In essence, they ask that the mayor and other officials come out from behind their documents, respecting them enough to address deeper 'truths' about the nature of the decision. This concern is only partially engaged by the mayor, who, at one point, admits the city's 'embarrassment' over the existence of a 'slum.'

The importance of land possession is a strong theme in both these interviews and older quotations. As one man noted, a slum is a place where people are renters and care little for the upkeep of the property, in contrast to hardworking Africville people for whom land and home ownership were symbols of pride and independence. As homeowners, he states, Africville residents were 'not second class citizens.' The film and subsequent book make it clear that the former residents' know that whites in positions of authority regarded them as incapable of self-determination, and their land as too valuable to remain 'black space.'

This concentrated series of commemorative events – the art exhibit, the documentary, the book, and the conference – marks an important turning point in the history of Africville's struggle. In effect, it begins a pedagogy that potentially transcends geographic and racial boundaries. Nowhere is this more apparent than in an excellent *Teacher's*

Guide, published in 1993 by a group of black and white educators, addressing the use of the film and book as educational resources in classrooms. Aimed at middle-high school students (approximately grades nine and ten), this guide suggests questions, classroom exercises, and assignments that challenge students to engage with the material within different subject areas.[11] For instance, the geography section involves an activity in which students reflect on the meaning of 'home' and what makes a community important to those who live there. They then trace the storyline told by former residents along the map of Africville provided in the book, identifying the location of specific homes and other sites. This section also introduces the concept of 'environmental racism,' and asks students to identify how Africville was deprived of services and targeted as a site of waste.

The economics exercises in the guide are designed to identify the poverty levels of Africville residents and spark discussion about the meaning of home ownership and personal property. The sociology section suggests students survey members of their community about their attitudes toward Africville, assessing whether or not the program of relocation was successful, and for whom. It also asks that students attempt to identify race and gender biases in the film and book, and in particular in the words of some white officials. In political science, they must discuss the access to power among different groups, the existence of racism in political systems, and the issue of appropriate redress for Africville residents.

While analysing the film and book, the student must consider questions such as: 'Whose voices, images and perspectives are heard/ absent?' 'Who is identified as an expert?' 'Who will benefit if we accept the story as it is expressed?' Overall, the guide is designed to engage the class in identifying the various interest groups – city council, the urban planners, the Africville residents, civil rights leaders, the outside Halifax community – and their particular investments in the Africville decision. It consistently develops an understanding of systemic racism as the basis for distinguishing between the interests, and the gains or losses, of these groups.

Both the documentary film and the book *The Spirit of Africville* depict the physical surroundings of the community. Students and other audiences are faced with a history that refuses fictionalization. Residents attest to both the good and the bad. While they are sometimes accused by other Haligonians of romanticizing Africville's life in hindsight,[12] for me, these works speak of unsurprising and realistic contradictions.

The community was in a beautiful site, yet was polluted by outside forces and unequipped to maintain itself well; residents had high levels of poverty, yet a strong sense of collective cooperation and support to help them survive. Interviewees do not feign a seamless, united voice, but speak of conflict and divides among community members, particularly when the city treated individuals differently. They acknowledge a degree of uncertainty in their feelings about relocation at the time, some younger members admitting they looked forward to what sounded like a wonderful new house and neighbourhood. Different expectations and high hopes hardly invalidate their loss.

Similar issues are addressed in an essay by Maureen Moynagh who theorizes Africville as, in Benedict Anderson's words, an 'imagined community.' By this she refers to the symbolic meaning the community engenders although it no longer exists in concrete form. Anderson's concept encompasses the broader meaning of nationalism, with the nation as an intangible idea held in common in the imaginations of its citizens. As Moynagh explains, 'Nationalism, then, is a simulacrum of community where not only geography but social difference effectively precludes that members should know one another or interact face to face.'[13] From such communities, people feel part of a larger body, garnering a particular identity in which to find pride and belonging. Moynagh's essay emphasizes the meaning Africville has come to hold for its residents and their descendants, not the matter of definable true conditions which may or may not be completely accurate in retrospect. Like Anderson, she holds that imagined community cannot be evaluated against real community, as its imagined status is 'a product of necessity not falsehood.'[14] She refers to theorist Gayatri Spivak's notion of 'strategic essentialism' as an approach to demands for justice and redress, positing that Africadian writers, like many in subjugated groups, reconstruct their community in fighting the pervasive racist discourses of the mainstream.

In Moynagh's analysis, black literature speaks back to a body of Nova Scotian folk culture centred around the histories of white settlers, and especially around the Celtic tradition. This dominant, white culture has been positioned by whites as the central identifying motif by which Nova Scotians both understand themselves and are understood by tourists and other outsiders. The recent rise in black cultural production challenges its hegemony by reminding the public of black history and white racism. Moynagh's analysis makes an important distinction between dominant forms of nationalism among majority groups and the strategic construction of nation in response to oppressive conditions. In this, the author is delineating a canon of works that challenge the erasure of violent histories and reaffirm black history and culture in the region.[15]

A recent play by George Boyd also portrays one black family's conflict over the prospect of leaving Africville. While the young woman is descended from generations of Africville people, her husband is a newcomer, there because of the marriage. He is amenable to the potentially profitable deals rumoured to be available from the city and to the modern opportunities an urban centre might offer, while she wishes to remain in her home. The play portrays the conflict between desires for upward mobility and for valued community traditions, as well as the meaning of place. When the young couple's baby dies from environmental contaminants, a dispute ensues as the city forbids them to bury the child in Africville, which is not 'consecrated ground.'[16]

While many works focus on black identity, Boyd's *Consecrated Ground* begins to address the inner complexities of white privilege and guilt through the prominent character of the white social worker. Entering with dreams of launching a noteworthy career through his rescue of the underclass, the social worker's consciousness develops as he begins to see the reality of what he has been sent to do.[17] While the young man is to perform the hands-on dirty work of his superiors, he is torn between the upward climb to inclusion in this elite group on the one hand, and his shame reflected in the face of black residents who, rather than depending on him, criticize and resent his involvement. When disillusioned about his former self-concept as saviour of the oppressed, he suffers something of an emotional breakdown and takes to drinking heavily. The viewer is asked to see the social worker not simply as a pawn of power, which he enacts with evil upon those 'below,' but as a complex characterization of the white subject's struggle to comprehend his position. We are left to ponder the ugliness upon which dominant identity rests, and, at the same time, a self-indulgent, fruitless guilt.

Consideration of this rich body of work raises the question of its reception in the dominant community. In light of my focus on both racial discourses and memory, it has been crucial to consider if, and how, the tone of discussion about Africville has changed in the white community in recent years. At first glance, it appears that some progress has been made. Black voices are no longer completely absent in the Halifax mainstream media; their messages are no longer uniformly portrayed as irrational or childlike protestations. An article such as Edna Staebler's would not likely appear in *Maclean's* today. Charles Saunders's careful following of Africville politics and related events is instead allowed a prominent place in Halifax papers. The commemorative art exhibit has toured the country, while poetry, the play, and public testimonies receive coverage in the local papers and the documentary has received nationwide acclaim. Clairmont and Magill's book *Life and Death* appeared in 1999 in its third edition, and annual Africville reunions on the former site have been taking place for years. Most liberal-leaning whites would acknowledge that mistakes were made in Africville, sometimes that the community's destruction was a tragedy. City officials have insisted that Africville would be treated quite differently today. Why, then, be concerned over its memory? Are these ideological shifts sincere or insufficient, and what might they really mean?

The mandate of this project is not to conduct a comprehensive survey of contemporary white attitudes about Africville, but several important observations can be made. Halifax has never formally or publicly apologized to Africville residents for the destruction of their community. New promises have been made and broken. City officials have abdicated responsibility for the past. Africville's space remains in control of the city of Halifax, which determines how it is to be used and enjoyed, as well as the educational message its memorial aspect conveys. The city has attempted to silence protests where possible, and criticized or dismissed them where visible. Although various commemorative works have permeated the mainstream community, perhaps tweaking the emotions of a guilty white public, Africville has not been incorporated in white Nova Scotia's history as a disgraceful fact of our past and present.[18]

Innocent Voices, Benevolent Forefathers

> The City of Halifax stands strong and proud that we're a good corporate community, and I don't think the city would treat their people unfairly. I don't think it's ever happened.
>
> Deputy Mayor of Halifax[19]

This statement in response to the Africville issue was made in 1994 by the deputy mayor; it can be interpreted in two ways. Either the city remains in complete denial that any mistakes were made in the treatment of Africville, or Africville residents are simply not considered to be 'the city's people.' Two related strands of examples attest to the fact that both assumptions are common among Halifax's governing body. First, racial discourse, that is, what the city *says* in response to Africville's questions and challenges, shows important similarities to the way these issues were treated in the 1960s. Where it has changed, the transformation is not necessarily more progressive but more a response to other social factors.

A conference documented in the film *Remember Africville* and the book *The Spirit of Africville* show former residents questioning the actions of city officials. Alternating footage of the contemporary dialogue and on-camera statements by officials from the time of Africville's destruction is revealing of how the story has been translated. Mayor Lloyd, in the 1960s, explains that, although 'you certainly don't coerce people ... people need to be shown things aren't in their best interests.' While former Mayor O'Brien is, in 1989, more careful, stating that things would be done more sensitively in the present, he reads a statement reciting the expert advice behind the city's decision. The text of his talk is published in full.[20] Perhaps most interesting is O'Brien's grappling with the official position on why the city wished to clear Africville land. He positions himself as a central decision maker, and clarifies that he has not come in a spirit of 'either pride or apology,' but to explain the way in which the city saw its actions at the time.

Speculation over the city's use of Africville land continued over time. The lingering rumours about residential or industrial development and a more recent one about the construction of the new Halifax–Dartmouth bridge all fed public confusion over a possible underlying motive. Industrial development ceased to be a concern as the relocation decision drew nearer, and O'Brien confirms this fact. He notes that many proposals passed by city council remained on paper only and were never put into effect. Similarly, he denied that the bridge construction was a factor, as officials at the time wished to place the bridge elsewhere, in the city's south end.[21]

O'Brien proceeds to compare the Africville relocation to that of a downtown area, in which low-income white residents had been forced out to make way for the Scotia Square shopping and office complex. Against this example, Africville is positioned as a more progressive and sensitive operation because a social worker was employed to oversee negotiation and because compensation was based, in his words, on 'need.' First, it is not clear how the involvement of the social worker, who was not a neutral party but worked for the city, made the process more just. Second, the former, downtown relocation was completed for a specific reason; no proposals for use of the Africville site were officially passed and little use has been made of it since. O'Brien obscures the fact that the white downtown residents were given a demonstrable explanation for their relocation – the mall was built, it does exist – while residents of Africville were left to wonder about various rumours and promised only improved living conditions, which they did not experience. Race, even as a relevant factor, is never mentioned.

O'Brien's speech manoeuvres to suggest alignment with the other side right after the opposite impression has been given. For example, immediately after arguing that Africville was treated better than the white downtown neighbourhood, he states, 'Maybe that does not sound right today and I agree that there is a lot about this that does not sound right today.'[22] This is nonsensical, as the original argument was designed to suggest the action was 'correct.' He then glosses his defence by moving immediately from the specific to the general, suggesting agreement on many other (unnamed) elements.

Racism does not factor in the explanation at any point although it is coded in the 'true' explanations offered. O'Brien admits the city's embarrassment over the so-called slum and cites a belief that integration and public housing would prevent the rise of 'ghettoes.' When the dialogue moves too close to race, however, the decision makers distance themselves from their task. Discomfort with the slum is said to have been a problem of 'the total Halifax community;' therefore, 'as a result, some action was pushed on us by that particular feeling.'[23] Social worker Peter MacDonald, speaking in the documentary film, *Remember Africville*, attempts to introduce a reversal of responsibility, similarly separating decision makers from the outcome of their actions. He states that 'you didn't go in and say, it's your day to move,' but that most such pressure came from within the community itself as neighbours began to leave. He does not address the forces under which neighbours left in the first place and upholds the notion that the city intended no harm. O'Brien ends his statement on a similar note – that of the unfortunate difference between the city's intended benevolent actions and their poor implementation.

In contrast, the other major white official involved in this conference speaks at some length of the mistakes and regrets of the city. Fred MacKinnon, who was deputy welfare minister at the time of relocation, stresses the importance of cultural identity and the need to honour the potential for survival and growth within existing communities. He critically compares the 'manipulation' of Africville to that of native children sent forcibly to residential schools and foster homes, projects in which he was also personally involved. He criticizes the lack of follow-up to the relocation, and the mistaken belief that culture and traditions could be transformed successfully from outside.

While these sentiments begin to suggest personal accountability and the desire for change, they are, at the same time, situated oddly in the context of this conference. MacKinnon is addressing an audience of many black former Africville residents who are angry, frustrated, and requesting explanations for what was done to them. In choosing to focus on the 'lessons' learned from Africville, he ends up proclaiming to this audience the approach that is needed when 'we' attempt to rescue an impoverished community. For instance, he states, 'I think we have to learn that many such communities, and Africville is a prime example, have a cultural identity, a personal identity and an emotional place in the hearts and minds of their people … I think the first fundamental lesson to be learned about such communities is that social and economic change cannot be manipulated.'[24] The lessons of which MacKinnon speaks are lessons for the white officials and decision makers of the city, as well as other outsiders who went along with relocation. Elements of such reflections would thus be useful in making a speech to council, but Africville residents hardly needed to learn these particular lessons. Further, such analysis is expressed in black critique and resistance; while the speaker may have rightfully listened and gleaned new perspectives from this, they are not of his own authorship.

Later MacKinnon states, 'Social and economic change for me personally, or for a community, has to begin not where you or someone else thinks that I should be … but where I am. Now you may not like where I am … but if you're going to effect social and economic change with me … you have to begin where I am.'[25] This positioning of identities – in an example where he is the oppressed and the Others are instructed in how to properly help him – reverses, thus obscures, the race relations being addressed. The speaker must perform these awkward discursive manoeuvres to lead the talk away from the accountability of whites, beginning with acknowledgment of who has erred, hinting at who has been wronged, but then reassembling the past into a generalized 'lesson for all.' Neither the bodies under discussion nor the bodies in the room have races. Africville residents are simply fellow citizens, coming to the discussion on a level playing field, learning their lesson alongside 'us.'

This passage indicates the ease with which well-meaning and regretful white authorities may unconsciously maintain a sense of 'us and them.' Though praising the community's own values, they still know best how these values are to be utilized. Similarly, they identify the attempted manipulation of other communities as something that 'doesn't work,' not something that is wrong or which officials had no business attempting in the first place.

Finally, even this more sensitive and thoughtful analysis assumes a project underscored by the good intent to make things better. It never addresses the racist discourses of the day, the complete lack of communication with the community, or the lack of attempt to instate viable plans. Regardless of MacKinnon's personal feelings at the time, or how those feelings materialize now that he has regrets, it is still dangerous to assume that the overall slant of the program was one of concern for the well-being of Africville and its people.

The frame within which we define what occurred also defines what questions can then be asked about it. The liberal framework of positive goals that simply 'didn't work' is so firmly entrenched that it is impossible for critics to meaningfully question the foundational intent. Residents, in this conference, *are* questioning the very foundation of the decision, of 'why they did what they did.' To answer this honestly would mean to state racism, to relinquish the 'good intent' foundation. No one in a position of authority has done this, which is why the answers are so rarely satisfying.

A 1994 document prepared by the Halifax director of social planning for city council echoes the responses to former residents recorded in the film and book. This study was prepared in response to two demands from the Africville Genealogical Society: the allotment of land for the rebuilding of the community's church[26] and the establishment of a scholarship fund for Africville descendants. Both requests are recommended to council in the report.

The report proceeds to review the 1960s decision and to justify the city's role. To this end it sets out to establish a 'context' in which the events must be placed. It states that the 'bulldozer approach' to social relocation was simply the accepted method of the day, and that the advice of 'experts' was the bedrock from which Africville was uprooted. While it claims today's approach would be 'more sensitive,' the older method is clearly justified in its day. The different options perceived at the time are reviewed and the final decision, that the city would use its statutory power but 'temper justice with compassion,' is again put forth. This establishes a particular tone, which reassures officials that their good intent has been acknowledged and is the foundation of all other discussion. They are said to have shown 'compassion' at all stages of the program and to have awarded compensation that was 'at least very fair and perhaps generous.' They are again reminded that the relocation program cost much more than the estimated cost at the time of planning, and this is upheld as evidence of generosity. This section concludes, simply, 'On compensation, the City did the right thing.'[27]

This report states various doubts as to the true nature of Africville, positing that memory has evolved into 'myths' of an idyllic, self-reliant community. These myths are deemed to have grown 'over time,' a conclusion that ignores the many examples of such community values, including some from the social worker and other outsiders, in the early *Relocation Report*. In addition, the report states that residents' impressions from the time about compensatory measures were misguided, since the city has no records of such promises. Concerns raised by residents about housing arrangements are recorded in the report, but never addressed, and what is called 'the education commitment' is said to have been solved through a small education fund and by giving former residents access to Halifax public schools. The latter is particularly absurd as Africville children had already attended Halifax schools for years. Further, public education is, by law, available to all children. This was hardly an extra reward.

The report's 'official story' concludes, 'The City of Halifax does need to recognize the reality of Africville in its history, celebrate the contributions the Africville people made to the City, and to continue to seek and help in their full participation in the life of the City.'[28] It then presents alternatives to the proposed plan, which include the options to review and revise it or to do nothing, which, it is warned, 'will likely contribute to the festering animosity between the descendants of the people of Africville and the City of Halifax. The City would also be left open to considerable negative publicity.'[29]

What *is* the reality of Africville in the city's history? How are the contributions to be celebrated, and how is full participation to be sought and supported? With neither further detail nor action, these phrases read like the vague rhetoric of the 1960s with its promises to 'take care' of residents for 'as long as necessary.' While the report takes pains to establish the context in which the decision was made, nowhere is the context of Africville's economic and physical demise discussed; nowhere is there room for assessment of the community's life and needs beyond a moment in the late 1960s, from a white perspective. The city's responsibilities are seen to begin and end with the purchase of land and the movement of people. 'The reality of Africville in the City's history,' from this document, is that of a problem that will not go away despite its fair and compassionate solution by the city. The compensation agreed to 'in principle'[30] can be considered a step forward, but it is awarded in the spirit of 'generosity' and the prevention of embarrassing conflict, not of regret or obligatory redress.

A further issue arose in 1994 over compensation when residents of Sackville, a community just outside Halifax, received reparation payments for living near a landfill site. Africville residents, who had lived much closer to their local landfill than many in Sackville, while suffering various other forms of pollution as well, began to ask why compensation had never been offered to them. A 'hotline' column in the *Halifax Daily News* posed the issue to the public. Haligonians could call in and record their opinions, which were then published in the next issue. This poll found that 77 per cent of callers (from a sample of 74) were against compensation for Africville. Some callers felt that Africville had already been adequately compensated. (Although, on the issue of the dump, no reparation had been made.) Other callers commented that Africville residents 'chose to live where the garbage was best,' that they were only 'squatters,' or that they had been 'savages.'[31]

Overall, responses to Africville's continued campaign have summoned the racial stereotypes, both implicit and explicit, of the 1950s and 1960s. The integration argument is common, exemplified in the conference speeches and in the 1994 words of Mayor Wallace, who stated, 'If Africville remained today, the city would be severely reprimanded for promoting segregation.'[32] As Genealogical Society president Irvine Carvery replied, other historically black communities remain, and are not seen to 'promote segregation.' The Society has been clear that a renewed residential community on the Africville site would not be black-only, nor would all former residents choose to move back; they would simply like first opportunity to re-establish themselves on the land, which would then be open to anyone.

However, the fear of outside perception remains, and other racial narratives repeat themselves when pressure becomes too forceful. Justifications today are barely more sophisticated than at the time, consisting of white-defined 'integration,' slum clearance, and the desires and fears of white citizens generally. The explanatory contexts articulate the concerns and positions of the dominant society, while

Africville's contextual story is dismissed as a romantic myth. Generosity, compassion, and justice remain in the fray, while historical distance allows both a lack of accountability and the construction of innocence in positing that we now have learned our lesson and would next time do it right. But if the major lesson learned is only that the former approach didn't work, what is to prevent the city's 'good intent' from reasserting itself in some new guise?

A Place to Dream Their Dreams

> The subject of the dream is the dreamer.
>
> Toni Morrison[33]

Seaview Park was established on newly groomed Africville soil in 1985, at a cost to taxpayers of approximately one million dollars. Although opposed by the current mayor and many members of council, its construction had been approved six years before by a different administration. Under pressure from a few north-end aldermen, it was built amid contention over the appropriate use of the space and ongoing pressures for industrial development.[34]

Seaview is an open field of low knolls with scattered young trees, gravel walking paths, and benches overlooking the water of the Bedford Basin. It has a paved parking lot and public washrooms. On the park's opening day, the deputy mayor of Halifax, who had fought for the park's existence, declared it a space 'for young and old, a place to dream their dreams,' thus Seaview was made a public site of recreation, open to 'everyone.' Former residents of Africville seemed conflicted over this designation. One woman present replied, 'Who wants to dream about uprooting people?' Others located the sites of their former homes and expressed sad memories. Some asked the obvious: if this money could be spent on the park, why couldn't Africville have been provided with services? Others conveyed a mix of regret and anger with a sense of satisfaction that at least Africville would be commemorated in its former space.[35] Regardless of their insights, fifteen years after the last Africville home was bulldozed, black space became 'public space,' a process described as the transformation of an eyesore. The city's Parks and Recreation Department received a Board of Trade landscape award for its work on the site.[36]

Despite some contradictory feelings, Seaview has become the site of the annual Africville reunion, at which former residents and their relatives meet for several days each summer. The gathering has included, over the years, picnics, parties, musical performances, church services, the launch of the book *The Spirit of Africville* and, in 2000, a wedding. A monument to Africville has been erected on the site as well, placed by the city in memory of the area's founding black families.

Although former residents have made the best of their park, its existence has met difficult times. Having achieved some measure of recognition of their story, the people of Africville and their few supporters in council were soon to realize their commemorative space was no more immune to the intrusion of commercial and industrial interests than had been their former community itself. In the early 1990s, the park became an object of renewed contestation when the city announced plans to build a new waterfront service road directly through the area. The road was to cross the exact sites of Seaview Church and the former elementary school, bisecting the land on which Africville residents were lobbying to one day rebuild the community.[37] Vigilant protest from former residents, now more organized than ever as the Africville Genealogical Society, took place over months, during which city officials voted down proposals for a public hearing on the issue and pressed the importance of the road for industrial development. The people of Africville finally achieved an agreement with the city by which the road would be rerouted around the park, and a replica of the church would be built on the site as a memorial. These accomplishments made the 1992 Africville reunion a cause for special celebration; it was attended by Martin Luther King III, who helped to break the ground where the new church was to stand.[38] To date, the park space has been preserved. Discussion of rebuilding the church, which was to be funded by the provincial government, surfaced throughout the 1990s, but action has never followed.

In 1994 there was a resurgence of contestation when two brothers, former Africville residents, occupied Seaview Park in support of ongoing demands for redress and renewed claims on the land. Victor and Eddie Carvery, who had been teenagers when forced to leave Africville, set up first a tent, and later two trailers, on the site of their former home, where they remained for the next several years. This action coincided with increased pressure on city hall from the Africville Genealogical Society to renegotiate with residents for compensation and related requests. Some demands included the employment of former Africville people in the park itself, and individual consideration for those who had received inadequate pay for their homes. Ultimately, the Africville activists wished to re-establish a community on the site. The brothers vowed to stay until an agreement was reached.

News reports of the time reflect a daily preoccupation with the presence of the Carverys in the park and cite complaints from other Halifax residents who claim the protest 'interferes with their enjoyment' of the space.[39] Mayor Fitzgerald had already threatened to evict them by force if necessary, although no law existed to justify this. The city had also locked the park's only washroom.[40] Some Haligonians angrily expressed a belief that the Carverys were receiving special treatment because of race,[41] ignoring the absurdity of such a remark given how Africville had been 'specially' treated because of race in the past.

In 1994, the Halifax city manager agreed to meet with Africville representatives to hear their requests and concerns. Covering this dialogue in the north end of the city, the media depicted the city manager as having been 'under fire' during a meeting 'dominated by anger and emotional outbursts.'[42] Another article describes the manager as having been 'under siege' and given a 'tongue-lashing.' The hostility and bitterness of the black community is central, and the article states, of Africville residents, 'None steered the session to collecting ideas, nor did they ask what residents should do to earn a sympathetic council ear.' In contrast, the city manager is the calm voice of reason; he is said to have 'led off the two-hour session by saying he hoped both sides could embark on a "co-operative venture" and not become confrontational.' Following his explanation to residents of the city's past 'fair and equitable' financial rewards, it is said that 'anger and venom flowed freely.' The article ends with a report of violence: in the preamble to a question, Eddie Carvery had been explaining his current welfare status, when another man in the audience interrupted and insulted him, stating that he did not pay his rent. Carvery, apparently, walked up to the man and punched him, then returned to his seat to finish his question as the other man was led out.[43]

I am not suggesting that an assault should be condoned, or ignored, by the media. However, in this context, a long and complex history of suspicion and denial of Africville's rights, complete with a personalized verbal attack in an emotionally charged meeting, were bound to have a provocative influence. Such background contexts are repeatedly omitted, leaving only an all-too-familiar image of black male violence.

The majority of news reports on Africville protests depict only the anger expressed by residents. Activists like Eddie Carvery are frequently belittled as irrate children who lack a reasonable analysis, much the way residents during the relocation era were deemed unable to comprehend their situation. Such reporting operates discursively to imprint black bodies with excessive emotion and anger, and white bodies with intellectual rationality.

When reference is made to the history behind protests, it is frequently in a doubtful tone, and is usually followed up by reports of some 'generous' action by the city. Regardless of the many different issues that arise over Africville, news reports repeatedly close with reminders of the same two concessions made by the city, sometimes with an interesting twist. For example, 'to appease former Africville residents council *decided* to provide land needed for the church and also plan to set up a $100,000 scholarship fund for Africville descendants [emphasis added].'[44] This completely overlooks the long fight residents had to gain these rewards, and that the building of the church had, at that time, already been delayed for several years. Many articles also close with reminders of the 1994 report on the city's alleged fairness and generosity toward Africville. A report of the north end meeting ends by citing the deputy mayor, who explains that the city has nothing to apologize for and simply has no money for this issue, thus there is no hope.

Commonly, white Halifax city councillors are portrayed as the rational, calm and understanding patriarchs, attempting to keep angry confrontations at bay. It seems that words about fairness and justice, spoken calmly or read from an 'official' document, cannot be understood as provocative of angry response. It is never noted that these participants in the discussion are not those whose history is being denied, and whose demands have rarely seen legitimate attention. Nor are they implicated in the same history that created Africville's situation in the first place. They do not have to ask permission to speak, or how to 'earn' a hearing of their concerns. They are not living in the aftermath of dislocation, on welfare, or in a cold public park. Yet in many reports they are portrayed as the victims of an angry black mob. And indeed, black anger appears an unforgivable threat, rarely with actual cause. Whether or not Carvery acted violently, then, I posit that such incidents cannot be considered and judged only in the moment they occur, out of time and space.

Although the Carvery brothers' campsite was at first patrolled by police, the city had no legal recourse to evict the protesters until it actively created some. This coincided with planning for the upcoming G7 Summit to be held in 1995, and many have speculated that the city feared embarrassment over its racial problem before an international audience.[45] Halifax was busily renovating the waterfront, creating parking space and beautifying the downtown, and meanwhile, realizing that its unsuccessful 1960s 'clean-up' of Africville had resurfaced: displaced residents had re-placed themselves. A few months before the summit, despite widespread protest from the black community, the city passed a bylaw that forbade citizens to camp in public parks overnight. Mayor Walter Fitzgerald cited the new ordinance as falling under the Protection of Property Act, announcing, *before the law was actually passed*, 'people are in the park illegally and we want them off.'[46] A letter to council from lawyers Burnley 'Rocky' Jones and Evangeline Cain-Grant, representing the Carverys, sums up the position of many blacks: 'the entire parks ordinance has apparently been manufactured around the objective of creating a legislative scheme to facilitate a second deportation of blacks from the Africville site and to suppress the protest of former Africville residents on the only occasion in many decades in which the international community will be focused on this city.'[47]

The passing of this ordinance sparked active protest in the black community, creating an apparent rift when the Africville Genealogical Society eventually supported the law. The difference in approach was reported in the media as divisive of the black community, and city councillors questioned whether the Genealogical Society was actually representative of Africville people. Irvine Carvery, society president and brother of Victor and Eddie, explained that the society did support his brothers' protest, although it was not the group's chosen strategy. They had felt compelled, however, to negotiate with the city in order to protect the rights of Africville residents to continue their annual reunions, which involved camping overnight in the park. This compromise resulted not in outright collaboration between the society and the city, as some suggested, but in an amendment to the bylaw that protected their right to hold the reunion.[48]

Protest against the bylaw from other activists received coverage in keeping with other depictions of disruptive and emotional blacks. The mayor, for instance, disciplined black spectators at the city hall meeting where the ordinance was passed. As the coverage reports:

'Speakers were allotted five minutes each and were signaled by the mayor when their time reached the last minute.' He also 'warned he would clear the council chambers if the Carverys' supporters didn't refrain from applauding speakers.'[49] A later article depicts angry protesters outside city hall, while stating that city officials, inside, were taking steps 'to repair relations with the descendants of Africville residents.'[50] These reparations consisted of the rezoning required to build Seaview Church, a promise by now several years overdue, and which was never carried out. Juxtaposed against the calm and benevolent, hardworking officials inside, the outside protests appear irrational and excessive.

During the week in which the city passed the bylaw to evict the Carverys, an anti-racism rally was held in celebration of the UN-declared International Day for the Elimination of Racial Discrimination. A media report, after describing speakers who 'bashed' city council over the new law, as well as some coverage of other issues relating to Africville and racism, again gave the mayor the final word: 'Mayor Walter Fitzgerald said yesterday the city is beefing up its anti-racism efforts.' The article proceeds to announce a city-sponsored series of anti-racism public service announcements in the works, and a committee on race relations that the mayor says 'is expected to become more active.'[51]

During the time of their occupation, news reports consistently portrayed subtle and not-so-subtle biases against the Carverys' protest. This was achieved partly through focus on other issues unrelated to their cause, for instance, rumours that the brothers had neglected their dogs who accompanied them at the site, complete with photos of the dogs' newborn puppies.[52] Another article closes with one line about how the park is being investigated as a popular cruising site for gay men. This appears completely out of the blue, rather than being, as one might expect, a separate issue worthy of another article. No effort is made to even suggest what it has to do with the Carverys and no particular news had developed in the 'ongoing' investigation. It does contribute to a general image of the park space as imperiled by yet another 'deviant,' unconstrained group.[53] A later article focuses specifically on the mess the campsite has caused, showing photos only of the protesters' garbage,[54] while others cite complaints from nearby residents about 'fish guts' left lying about, and the condition of the brothers' trailers.[55]

Despite these conditions, which the Carverys denied, Mayor Fitzgerald announced that he would not evict them immediately after passing the new legislation. Again, reports position the mayor as patient and understanding, and quote him as saying that the city has been sympathetic and fair in attempts to negotiate this sensitive terrain. He is allowed to correct any misconceptions the public might have of the term 'racism,' which he claims is used too frequently: 'I think it's a few people who didn't get their way and they yell "racism" ... There's not a shred of racism in this. They're entitled to their opinion – even if they're wrong.' Still, the mayor positions himself as fair and open-minded, stating, 'if they can show us that we haven't given every sensitivity to this and bent over backwards, then that's something.'[56] Similarly, the alderman who reported the above complaints from area residents stated, 'Everybody is human – I understand how they feel ... But they have to understand that 30 years ago and now are two different times.'[57]

Shortly after passing the new law, the city gave the Carvery brothers a notice of eviction. However, the city's plans appeared to backfire somewhat: the brothers moved their protest just outside the park's border, to an area that did not fall under municipal jurisdiction.[58] Here, the Carverys noted to reporters, their presence was actually more visible, in contrast to their camp at the back of the park away from the main roads. As the city alone could not evict them without provincial and federal consent, they remained there for several more years. The mayor's application to the provincial and federal governments remained unanswered for some time.

During 1996, Eddie Carvery was arrested after a conflict with environmental consultants working in Seaview Park.[59] He was alleged to have argued with and threatened them, as well as to have threatened damage to their equipment and vehicles. Coverage of this issue was detailed and emphatic; Carvery did not plead guilty and was given a year's probation after his trial. He and Victor maintained their campsite until, in February of 1999, Eddie Carvery fell ill and was unable to stay there. As Charles Saunders reports, 'When he returned, he found that his camper, tent and boat had vanished. He went to the city to find out what had happened to his property, and was eventually directed to a warehouse that later burned to the ground. When he asked for redress, or even an explanation, he says he was told to "get a lawyer."'[60]

By 1996, having found little success in attempted negotiations, the Africville Genealogical Society had finally gathered the resources to launch a law suit against the City of Halifax with the Supreme Court of Nova Scotia, demanding compensation for the current value of their lands.[61] While details are difficult to locate, it appears to have been held up by lack of funding, difficulties in obtaining city records, and legal red tape. The suit has yet to be resolved.

The city's dealings with the Carverys and other protesters, and its establishment and 'defence' of Seaview Park, are not unique. Urban space in white settler societies is not easily occupied by dominated, displaced people. Particularly when such groups organize to demand reparations, to have their rights recognized, or simply to tell their histories through public installations, the disruption is often perceived as an invasion of both space and established white knowledge. Employing Lefebvre's concept of 'abstract' space, Eugene McCann discusses how the central urban spaces where business and government operate are made to appear 'neutral,' orderly, and free from conflict, often at the expense of racialized and poor groups whose housing is razed to make way for office towers and other commercial interests. Further, it often results in their ultimate exclusion from the sphere that is purported to be 'public,' and positions them as disruptive of the normal day-to-day functioning of dominant society. As Lefebvre asserts, 'abstract' space is that without a history; it has been established, in opposition to the 'concrete' spaces of people's everyday lives and experiences, as space with a set of consensual assumptions about what is to take place within it. It is supposed to be non-violent, trouble-free, safe for business people to conduct their affairs. Highlighting these assumptions, McCann studies the shooting of an unarmed black man by a white police officer in Lexington, Kentucky, and the subsequent protests by black residents, which moved at one point to the central business district. These demonstrations interrupted dominant conceptions of what safe, orderly, abstract public space is supposed to mean, and to whom it is available. McCann demonstrates how the racial geography of the city structured the shock and outrage of white, middle class citizens when their space was invaded by anger and frustration that is presumed to be contained in the racialized ghettoes.[62]

Similarly, Samira Kawash demonstrates that the designation of public space is a system of inclusion and exclusion in her study of 'the homeless body.'[63] She discusses how public amenities are closed to those who live on the street and in public parks as a way of banning unwanted, and unentitled, bodies. This is accomplished through by-laws that regulate, for instance, panhandling and sleeping in public, and that lock public parks and washrooms, often with the backing of neighbourhood groups. The homeless, then, can exist 'nowhere,' and these processes of eviction serve to constitute the bodies and spaces of entitlement through the production of the degenerate and restricted.

The Carverys' protest, and black protests and meetings elsewhere in Halifax, contested the dominant management of space in different ways. Public protests inserted black bodies into the abstract spaces of downtown, city hall, and formal meetings. At the same time, in many instances they failed to behave as white authorities demanded and as white norms dictated. This had the effect of disruption, but also of eliciting specific representational practices on the part of the media. By examining how 'different' behaviour was received and presented in 'respectable' space – as uncontrolled rage and irrationality – it is possible to see how racial narratives inform every facet of each encounter, as well as the widespread images produced in its aftermath.

The Carverys, on the other hand, reclaimed their homeplace on site, and their presence challenged the way in which space had been restructured to hide the evidence of past violences. These violences were again brought to the attention of the Halifax community at large. When viewed in a critical light, the citizen and government resistance to this uncovering of history is instructive: again, whites rushed to discredit dissenting voices by rendering them degenerate, irrational, and violent. Dominant accounts suggested that the blacks who reoccupied the space were effectively reproducing the slum that the city had dealt with thirty years before. As these narratives are so congruent with how Africville residents have always been depicted, it is extremely difficult to imagine that a similar eviction would never take place again.

Conclusion: Monumental Space

> Such a space is determined by what may take place there, and consequently by what may not take place there.
>
> Henri Lefebre[64]

In 1998, Seaview Park was endowed with an important symbolic honour when the Historic Sites and Monuments Board of Canada named it a site of historical significance for a cultural community. While a crucial step to establishing Africville's history in the consciousness of the nation, symbolic moves are questionable when they remain unaccompanied by the political will to make good on long overdue promises. In other words, we should interrogate the conditions under which remembering is possible, and thus, the very integrity of the historical project and its projected lessons. Andreas Huyssen, writing of commemorative sites in urban centres, is concerned with the public representation of historical trauma, in particular with the growth of a global 'cultural obsession' over memory in the last three decades. What does it mean, he wonders, that we increasingly memorialize traumatic events, bringing them effectively into the present? To what (political, social, personal) ends do we review, commodify, interpret, and employ memory? How and to what ends do we struggle to distinguish 'real' or authentic memory from the various permutations of media representation that bring the past increasingly to our fingertips? Huyssen posits that the recent cultural incitement to remember history is simply the other side of the coin on which historical amnesia is imprinted. Further, memory is, of course, inherently contingent and dynamic; in Huyssen's words it is 'haunted by forgetting, in brief, human and social. As public memory it is subject to change – political, generational, individual. It cannot be stored forever, nor can it be secured by monuments.'[65]

Monumental space, in Africville's case, can in fact mask events in its apparent homage to the black community. It can be seen to replace material gains and to compensate for the past, symbolizing a reunion of communities. This space, too, is premised on the particular manner in which the space is to be used, even if its dictates remain tacit: Celebrations of black culture that are positive and joyful in tone, such as annual reunions, are allowed. Protests that criticize the city's actions are not, particularly those that violate notions of the civilized use of public space. Africville's demise can be mourned, racism can occasionally be noted as a phenomenon. It must not, however, be attached to specific bodies or groups. Its deliberate enactment cannot be named. Monumental space can present a newly scripted story of its contents, which is, in keeping with its public nature, palatable to the majority.

While its meaning for the black community might be clear, a white outsider, or anyone unfamiliar with Africville's history, would encounter few clues in the park to indicate how the space has become what it is today. The large monument in the shape of a sundial marks the former site of Africville's church. It is inscribed on one side with the surnames of former residents, and on the other as follows:

Seaview Memorial Park
land deeded
1848–1969

Dedicated in loving memory of
the first black settlers and all
former residents of the community
of Campbell Road, Africville and all
members of the Seaview United
Baptist Church

First Black Settlers
William Brown
John Brown   Thomas Brown

'To lose your wealth is much
To lose your health is more
To lose your life is such a loss
that nothing can restore'

Africville families have regarded this as their monument; it is understandably important as a rare acknowledgment of black space, community, and roots. Still, its message is perplexing. For instance, except
in a few cases, Halifax never recognized the land as having been
deeded to black settlers, and none received treatment in line with this
assumption. It is unclear whose loving sentiment is represented here,
as history obviously attests to a quite different view of blacks by
whites. The rather odd final stanza suggests a loss of human life, rather
than of a community, and never suggests how this came about. What is
an outsider to make of this message? Perhaps that the early black
settlers, the other former residents, and the church members were
summarily wiped out in some unnamed natural disaster?

Just as the subject of the dream is the dreamer, the subject of memory
is the one who remembers. Perhaps if one comes to the park as a
former resident or a descendant, or as one in whom the story of racism
has been instilled as an organizing principle of one's history, the monument needs no further clarification. However, what of those who come
to the site as a place where they once dumped their garbage? What of
those who 'knew' Africville through newspaper reports as a dangerous slum by the dump? What of the tourist who leaves thinking of

Halifax as a 'strong and proud' community that has never 'treated its people unfairly,' and has kindly chosen to honour its founding black families? And what of the memory of those who were instrumental in the destruction of Africville?[66] Multiple projections of memory are possible, contingent upon the particular identities of visitors. All bring specific conceptual tools and histories to the open air of the park and the foot of the monument. What, we might then ask, is the pedagogical potential of such a public site for those whose re-education is crucial?

Jane Jacobs has examined public memorials and commemorative spaces in white settler societies. She explores the contemporary narrative of 'reconciliation' that underpins the public positioning of histories. In its attempt to unite historically colonized and colonizing groups under a common national identity, reconciliation 'attempts to bring the nation into contact with the "truth" of colonisation – and this includes the attendant emotional "truths" of guilt, anger, regret and hurt – in order that there might be a certain "healing."'[67] In Jacobs's Australian study, reconciliation is a government-sponsored discourse; elite political figures determine its meaning and the events and artifacts through which it will be articulated. While some projects are meted out to Aboriginal people, they are necessarily compromised when the government has final say in the narrative. This becomes apparent in the settings and censorship of these efforts.

Jacobs examines 'countermonuments' as efforts to tell a marginalized perspective alongside or in place of traditional forms. For instance, she considers an 'Aboriginal walking tour' in the city of Melbourne, in which new monuments have been placed near existing colonial memorials, challenging the hegemonic story of the discovery and settlement of Australia by white Europeans. While many such monuments present critical challenges, they have been constructed within the bounds of municipal government approval. Some monuments, felt to depict too much violence, were censored, while others were allowed only in particular sites away from the central downtown region where they would receive the most exposure. Jacobs notes how the creative licence of Aboriginal artists was limited by the collaborative nature of the project, and how the monuments are situated subtly, so that one must seek out the walking trail and read the accompanying brochure to understand their intent. Unlike the imposing and central colonial monuments, one must consciously solicit the knowledge of an Other history.

Similarly, Africville's monument is contained in one site, and great effort has been spent in city attempts to manage its narrative. In this, it is unconnected to the decision-making council in downtown Halifax, the offices of the mayor, development officer, other officials, or social workers. It remains in an underutilized park in an area of the city known as dangerous. Even here, it does not tell the full story of relocation. Like the Aboriginal walking trails, its message is limited pedagogically.

Huyssen, too, points to the limitations of present-day notions of reconciliation and their embodiment in counter-monuments or other alternative forms. He explores several sites at which artists creating memory installations, in the form of parks, buildings, and monuments, have grappled with the problem of how to effectively convey memory, attempting to 'evade the fate of imminent invisibility.'[68] Underlying this struggle, he suggests, is the challenge of establishing monumental spaces that promote the inscription of past atrocities in the national consciousness (in his work, for example, the Holocaust, the Argentinean state's terror against the *desaparecidos*, and the World Trade Center attacks). Notwithstanding the complexities of achieving public memory consensus, particularly in light of intra-national histories, he notes that 'by resisting the desire to forget, the memorial as a site of intervention in the present may become an agent of political identity today.'[69] And indeed, for former Africville residents, such meaning is potentially offered in Seaview Park. At the same time, the space exudes a sense of disconnection from the life of the city; it does not seem part of an archival network of relationships among events, groups, histories that would allow Africville a meaningful niche in the nation's ownership of a violent and racist past. In addition, monumental space, as any space, does not simply exist, static and untouched by social and political processes. It would seem impossible, for instance, to divorce any consideration of the park's significance today from either the Carverys' troubled history of re-eviction or the ongoing absence of white accountability in Africville's story.

Jane Jacobs, referring to the 'regulated geographies' of Aboriginal Australia, points to how space itself is the forum through which 'subversive' stories are managed or suppressed.[70] Nowhere is this more apparent than in Seaview Park, where history is put to rest, held down by the monument, while black protest must be silenced and banished. Like the Carverys and their supporters, protesting Aborigines in Jacobs's analysis are depicted as 'invading' white space; clearly their history does not belong in the urban landscape.

Despite its limited scope, the discourse of reconciliation raises great anxieties among non-Aboriginals as to their understandings of their past and their place in the nation's history. This, in Jacobs's analysis, has served to rekindle a more overt racism imbued with a sense that Aboriginal people now possess too much power and privilege. Would attempts to retell the truth of Africville's history in the public forum result in a similarly defensive hostility? Does the monument, along with more recent acceptance of memorials in the form of plays, music, and art displays, incur a sense of reconciliation among white Haligonians, a sense that they have gone far enough in paying tribute to 'unfortunate' events of the past?

Halifax too has seen the appearance of heightened resentment toward Africville residents' demands at the governmental level – in assertions that the city has been generous and compassionate where to begin with there has been no racism. This comes after relatively little visible disruption, considering that the camp protest was confined mainly to the park, and the rather mild memorial symbols that are contained in that space. Still, as the former residents' requests plod forward, delayed over years, white tolerance for the issues seems to recede more and more into a sense that blacks simply cannot put the past in the past. It is easy to overlook that the extensive coverage of the issues does not equal an abundance of new gains and privileges: in other words, the fact that we seem to hear about it over and over for years does not mean that anything has changed or progressed. A sense exists, however, that this is the case; white fears and anxieties are supported by common media representations showing the 'anger' and implying the potential violence of black activists. The view that blacks have received ample compensation already is no doubt bolstered by the constant repetition of the same few concessions granted by the city, with little follow-up as to whether they have actually been carried out. There is little to combat these narratives in the daily lives of most whites. News and events presented in the easiest and most pervasive forms of consumption portray such dominant images.

The park and monument to Africville residents and their early forebears cannot be devalued. It is significant in any North American urban centre that black settlers should be honoured and remembered, that space, which was once black space, should be memorialized. It has come to stand for much more than destruction and grief – for change, resistance, and the commitment to seeing that history is not repeated. However, the meaning attached to any public object is different according to one's history and subject position. As an educational and commemorative tool for the white community, indeed for anyone new to Africville's story, the monumental space tells little. It can appear to be the mark of a city that values its black history, or that simply chooses to honour the home of original blacks, whose descendants were successfully integrated into the rest of the community, thus symbolizing the progress for which the relocation was supposed to stand.

A dominant community forms not through exclusionary practice alone, but through, to borrow Sibley's term, 'geographies of exclusion.' It is the acts of burial – indeed, a monument seeks to 'put to rest' – and of forgetting, which form a link in the chain of ongoing evictions of Africville from its own space. Through the desecration of space that is black, the appropriation of space to become white, the suppression of the story of this violence, and the denial of accountability, the life of Africville remains grounded upon a geography of racism and its discursive organization. Like the proverbial lie, once told, the story necessitates the telling of a chain of maintenance fictions, complete with the management of space in such a way that the fictions prevail intact and that oppositional stories remain buried.

On the surface, reconciliation insists that space can be rescripted as something new and inclusive. 'A place to dream their dreams' is a place given citizens by a caring municipality that appreciates its diverse history and cultivates the future hopes and aspirations of all. This municipality struck down racial apartheid in decades past, drawing frightened blacks from self-imposed isolation, while the rest of society awaited their contributions. These dreams do not include the nightmares of poverty, destruction, and expulsion, nor the hopes of reparation and a chance to improve the future. These dreams are costly to some; they are premised on forgetting what is buried, on retelling how this place has become what it is. Dreams may take place in this monumental space, but some dreams may not be spoken. We cannot be reconciled to this.

Afterword

Reflections on 9/10–9/11

The day after I defended my doctoral dissertation – the original version of this book – the World Trade Center towers were attacked. I had slept fitfully on the night of September 10, with the questions of my examining committee still ringing in my head in the twisted and confused way of dreams. I slept later than usual in the morning, trying to realize some degree of closure. I awoke to a different world.

Of course, it wasn't really a different world. It was a dramatic and jarring realization of a history in the making. But it was a day that seemed to catalyse a new era, in the very proximity of an enemy that had always been constructed as from elsewhere – from a place that wasn't quite real. The enemy was now within and 'we,' secure North Americans, knew that our borders would not retain the old meanings we thought we had known. This enemy was more terrifying than we could have imagined, packaged on our nightly news and in our daily papers as barely human. Moreover, we were told, he could be the corner dry-cleaner, the neighbour across the street, a school friend of your child.

Canadians on the left were quick to oppose what we saw as widespread American self-righteous innocence, and fearfully alarmed by the multitude of reactive racist outpourings that seemed to compose the very air we breathed – physical and verbal attacks on Muslims, harassment at the border, the vandalism of mosques, human excrement left on a friend's doorstep. These things were chilling in their proximity as well. It seemed crucial to don a political shield against the insidious fear mongering. But still, did we not think twice on the subway? Did we never glimpse the CN Tower through the downtown Toronto smog of September and wonder 'what next'? This turning point delivered, in some ways, a virulent new articulation of racialized fear, while drawing on the oldest narratives: us and them, east and west, barbaric and civilized, democratic and fundamentalist, brown and white. We have since seen terrifying new wars, newly intensified efforts at policing the border, new regimes of torture – which are also reliant on the oldest narratives.

All this is certainly not to suggest that anti-black racism in Halifax/ Africville can be directly compared to anti-Arab sentiment in the world at large, or to suggest any simplistic links between them. But what has come about in the last five years is a newly cemented culturalized racism, with deeply intensified notions of the lines between the Other and Us. Discourses of national belonging and the rightful occupancy of nation and place are infused with more than resentment or intolerance; they are saturated in fear. This fear has taken a very particular shape under the auspices of security and protection – a shape that makes the naming of racism nearly impossible. Abhorrence of the Other is now justified in our national discourse; protection and security are merely necessary. It is easy to say we don't mean 'all Muslims,' but it is only rational, after all, to defend against the *irrational*. Racism need not come into the equation at all.

Razing and Racing History

Around the time I began revising this version of the book in 2006, two important black heritage sites in Nova Scotia were firebombed. The Black Cultural Centre in Dartmouth was attacked with six Molotov cocktails, resulting in extensive damage. Within two months of that incident, the Black Loyalist Heritage Society's office at Birchtown was burned to the ground.[1]

Responding to these incidents, black community members, as well as the RCMP officers investigating the case, were called upon to speculate about the existence of ongoing racist violence in Nova Scotia, to posit *yes* or *no* to various permutations of the query, 'Is it possible … still … in 2006?' When regarded in historical context, there is more than good reason for the community to experience these attacks as racially targeted. Their felt impact can hardly be minimized.

Perhaps more illuminating than the fact of ongoing racism – in Nova Scotia or anywhere – is the particular form these attacks took:

they were not against individuals or homes, but against heritage sites, repositories of cultural artifacts and documents. They were the spaces, the archives, in which history is housed, where it is recorded, preserved, and called upon. Assuming these were indeed racist hate crimes, attempts to eradicate culture at its cradle, they speak of a particularly focused violence. It is one that threatens to delegitimize the very claim to existence – to history, to place – of a community: There are no records. (Haven't we heard this before?) There were no deeds. There was no documentation. The 'promises' were not recorded in the minutes.

The consequences of such eradication are no great mystery, just as the ongoing-ness of hatred should not continue to surprise us in a climate in which we are taught to fear both internal and external enemies. No matter the extent of place and history, those who are racialized are assured no measure of belonging.

Razing – of places, buildings, records, cultures – requires forgetting. And like erasure, forgetting requires substantial work. It requires legislation, the resurfacing of landscapes, careful wording. To resist forgetting is to refuse the official story of benevolent intent, of 'mistake,' and of reconciliation. It is also to regard the difficult, the painful, the ugly as part of history – to talk about it, to debate it, to move with it, and beyond it at once. Legal theorist John Calmore writes, 'There is … no euphemistic, polite way to say what must be said about racism.'[2] Indeed, a set of implicit rules seems to govern any such discourse, and too often they position 'racism' as simply a word appropriated by white people to denote an insult to our persons, an (implicitly unfair) accusation. Refusing these rules involves naming racism in the present tense, even in reference to groups or governing bodies, not as something subsumed in extreme and temporally contained phenomena like slavery and war, but as a structural feature of society, and as an organizing principle of knowledge and politics. Presently, it also calls for an intensified critique of what is constructed as culturally inspired terror threatening our borders and the very seat of our own Western identities.

I leave open-ended the question of how accountability might be fostered in this climate, and of how issues of reparation might be seriously regarded by dominant white players at this stage in Africville's history. These are questions implied throughout this work, and they are ongoing for former residents, their allies, and those they challenge. At the crux of such a struggle lies the incentive to theoretically rethink the case, to demonstrate harm, and to contest innocence. Refusing the official story means desisting in appropriating Africville's demands as insults to white pride. The story of Africville is not one of white pain. It is a story of white erasure and forgetting. If such a story can be disrupted in concrete social and legal spaces, perhaps its geography need not stay buried in the soil of Africville.

Notes

1 Authoring Africville: A Selected History

1 See, for example, Jeffery Burton, *Confinement and Ethnicity: An Overview of World War II Japanese American Relocation Sites* (Seattle: University of Washington Press, 2002); Roger Daniels, *Japanese Americans: From Relocation to Redress* (Seattle: University of Washington Press, 1991); Frank Iritani, *Ten Visits: Brief Accounts of Our Visits to All Ten Japanese American Relocation Centers of World War II …* (San Mateo, CA: Japanese American Curriculum Project, 1994); Harold S. Jacoby, *Tule Lake: From Relocation to Segregation* (Comstock: Bonanza Press, 1996); Charles McClain, ed., *The Mass Internment of Japanese Americans and the Quest for Legal Redress* (New York: Garland, 1994); Mona Oikawa, 'Cartographies of Violence: Women, Memory, and the Subject(s) of the "internment"' (PhD diss., University of Toronto, 1999); Page Smith, *Democracy on Trial: The Japanese-American Evacuation and Relocation in World War II* (New York: Simon & Schuster, 1995).
2 Joy Bilharz, *The Allegany Senecas and Kinzua Dam: Forced Relocation through Two Generations* (Lincoln: University of Nebraska Press, 1998).
3 Ila Bussidor, *Night Spirits: The Story of the Relocation of the Sayisi Dene* (Winnipeg: University of Manitoba Press, 1997). See also, René Dussault, *The High Arctic Relocation: A Report on the 1953–55 Relocation* (Ottawa: Royal Commission on Aboriginal Peoples, 1994); Alan Marcus, *Out in the Cold: The Legacy of Canada's Inuit Relocation Experiment in the High Arctic* (Copenhagen: IWGIA, 1992); Alan Marcus, *Relocating Eden: The Image and Politics of Inuit Exile in the Canadian Arctic* (Hanover, NH: Dartmouth College, 1995); Frank Tester, *Tammarniit (Mistakes): Inuit Relocation in the Eastern Arctic, 1939–63* (Vancouver: UBC Press, 1994).

4 See, for instance, John Bauman, *Public Housing, Race, and Renewal: Urban Planning in Philadelphia, 1920–1974* (Philadelphia: Temple University Press, 1987); Howard Gillette, *Between Justice and Beauty: Race, Planning, and the Failure of Urban Policy in Washington, DC* (Baltimore: Johns Hopkins University Press, 1995); Arnold R. Hirsch, 'Containment on the Home Front: Race and Federal Housing Policy from the New Deal to the Cold War,' *Journal of Urban History* 26, no. 2 (2000): 158–89; Arnold R. Hirsch, *Making the Second Ghetto: Race and Housing in Chicago, 1940–1960* (Cambridge: Cambridge University Press, 1983); Liam Kennedy, *Race and Urban Space in Contemporary American Culture* (Edinburgh: Edinburgh University Press, 2000); Joe W. Trotter and Tera Hunter, eds., *African American Urban Experience: Perspectives from the Colonial Period to the Present* (New York: Palgrave Macmillan, 2004). For a discussion of the British context, see Jeffrey Henderson, *Race, Class, and State Housing: Inequality and the Allocation of Public Housing in Britain* (Aldershot, Hampshire: Gower, 1987). For an overview of international literature, see Scott Leckie, 'Forced Evictions,' *Environment and Urbanization* 6, no. 1 (1994): 131–46.

5 Arnold R. Hirsch, 'Searching for a "Sound Negro Policy": A Racial Agenda for the Housing Acts of 1949 and 1954,' *Housing Policy Debate* 11, no. 2 (2000): 393–441.

6 James Robert Saunders and Renae Nadine Shackelford, *Urban Renewal and the End of Black Culture in Charlottesville, Virginia: An Oral History of Vinegar Hill* (Jefferson, NC: McFarland, 1998).

7 P.R. Mullins, 'Engagement and the Color Line: Race, Renewal, and Public Archaeology in the Urban Midwest,' *Urban Anthropology* 32, no. 2 (2003): 205–30.

8 Harvey K. Newman, 'Race and the Tourist Bubble in Downtown Atlanta,' *Urban Affairs Review* 37, no. 3 (2002): 301–21.

9 See also Kevin Fox Gotham, 'A City without Slums: Urban Renewal Public Housing and Downtown Revitalization in Kansas City, Missouri,' *American Journal of Economics and Sociology* 60, no. 1 (2001): 285–316; Brett Williams, 'A River Runs through Us,' *American Anthropologist* 103, no. 2 (2001): 409– 31.

10 Bridglal Pachai, *Beneath the Clouds of the Promised Land: The Survival of Nova Scotia's Blacks*, vol. 1 (Halifax: Black Educators Association of Nova Scotia, 1987), 30–1.

11 Ibid., 44.

12 Daniel N. Paul, *We Were Not the Savages* (Halifax: Nimbus, 1993).

13 Six years following their arrival, only 14 per cent of blacks had received land grants at all. Pachai, *Beneath the Clouds*, 47, 46.

14 C.B. Fergusson, *A Documentary Study of the Establishment of the Negroes in
Nova Scotia between the War of 1812 and the Winning of Responsible Government*
(Halifax: Public Archives of Nova Scotia, 1948), 8–9; Pachai, *Beneath the
Clouds*; John N. Grant, *Black Nova Scotians* (Halifax: Nova Scotia Museum,
1980), 20.

15 Birchtown was one of the largest settlements of blacks outside Africa
at the time, with a population of about 1500. Pachai, *Beneath the Clouds*,
47–8.

16 See Sheridan Hay, 'Black Protest Tradition in Nova Scotia: 1783–1964'
(master's thesis, Saint Mary's University, 1997).

17 James W. St G. Walker, 'The Establishment of a Free Black Community
in Nova Scotia, 1783–1840,' in *The African Diaspora: Interpretive Essays*,
ed. Martin L. Kilson and Robert I. Rotberg (Cambridge, MA: Harvard University
Press, 1976), 214; T. Watson Smith, 'The Slave in Canada,' *Collections
of the Nova Scotia Historical Society*, vol. 10 (Halifax: Nova Scotia Printing
Company, 1899).

18 Cited in Donald H. Clairmont and Dennis W. Magill, *Nova Scotian Blacks:
An Historical and Structural Overview* (Halifax: Institute of Public Affairs,
Dalhousie University, 1970), 29.

19 Highlighting an apparently common white view, the Earl of Dalhousie,
Governor of Nova Scotia, wrote 'slaves by habit and education, no longer
working under the dread of the lash, their idea of freedom is idleness and
they are therefore quite incapable of industry.' Ibid., 30.

20 Walker, 'Free Black Community,' 212–13.

21 Mary Casey, 'Africville Awaits the Wreckers,' *Globe and Mail*, 25 August
1962; Frank Doyle, 'Africville: 3-Sided Question,' *Halifax Mail Star*, 5 February
1963; Barbara Hinds, 'Africville Families Poisoned,' *Halifax Mail Star*,
28 January 1958.

22 Throughout the book, I often avoid use of the term 'relocation,' except
when referring to how the city viewed its own policy for it denotes a politically
benign arrangement in which all parties simply agree to the movement
of persons. I frequently use more realistic terms like 'destruction,'
'removal,' or 'forced relocation.'

23 Marianne W. Jørgensen and Louise Phillips, *Discourse Analysis as Theory and
Method* (London: Sage, 2002); Teun A. van Dijk, 'Media Discourse,' in *Sage
Series on Race and Ethnic Relations*, ed. John H. Stanfield II (Newbury Park,
CA: Sage, 1993).

24 Oscar Lewis, *La Vida: A Puerto Rican Family in the Culture of Poverty –
San Juan and New York* (New York: Random House, 1966). Lewis is noted for
various studies of Mexican families, for example, *The Children of Sanchez:*

Autobiography of a Mexican Family (New York, Vintage Books, 1961), *Five Families: Mexican Case Studies in the Culture of Poverty* (New York: Basic Books, 1959).

25 Bob Carter, *Realism and Racism: Concepts of Race in Sociological Research* (London: Routledge, 2000), 28.

26 For further explanation, see Graham Burchell, Colin Gordon, and Peter Miller, eds., *The Foucault Effect: Studies in Governmentality* (Chicago: University of Chicago Press, 1991); Michel Foucault, *Power/Knowledge: Selected Interviews and Other Writings,1972–1977*, ed. Colin Gordon (New York: Pantheon Books, 1980).

27 Jørgensen and Phillips, *Discourse Analysis*.

28 Stuart Hall, 'The Work of Representation,' in *Representation: Cultural Representations and Signifying Practices*, ed. S. Hall (London: Sage Publications, 1997), 45.

29 Bronwyn Davies, 'The Subject of Post-Structuralism: A Reply to Alison Jones,' *Gender and Education* 9, no. 3 (1997): 272.

30 Michel Foucault, 'Two Lectures,' in *Power/Knowledge: Selected Interviews and Other Writings, 1972–1977*, ed. C. Gordon (New York: Pantheon Books, 1972), 97.

31 Judith Butler, *Bodies that Matter* (New York: Routledge, 1993).

32 See Michael Taussig, 'Culture of Terror – Space of Death: Roger Casement's Putumayo Report and the Explanation of Torture,' in *Violence in War and Peace: An Anthology*, ed. Nancy Scheper-Hughes and Philippe Bourgeois (Malden, MA: Blackwell, 2004), 40.

33 For instance, First Nations in North America still experience a largely colonial style of administration. See Sherene H. Razack, 'Gendered Racial Violence and Spatialized Justice: The Murder of Pamela George,' *Canadian Journal of Law and Society* 15, no. 2 (2000): 91–130; Dara Culhane, *The Pleasure of the Crown: Anthropology, Law and First Nations* (Burnaby, BC: Talon Books, 1998).

34 David Theo Goldberg, *Racist Culture, Philosophy and the Politics of Meaning* (Oxford: Blackwell, 1993), 187.

35 For discussion of the role of geography in constructing race and gender as social categories, see Audrey Kobayashi and Linda Peake, 'Unnatural Discourse. "Race" and Gender in Geography,' *Gender, Place and Culture* 1, no. 2 (1994): 225–43.

36 Barbara Fields, *Slavery and Freedom on the Middle Ground* (New Haven: Yale University Press, 1982), 151.

37 Michael Omi and Howard Winant, "Racial Formation," in *Race Critical Theories*, ed. Philomena Essed and David Theo Goldberg (Malden, MA: Blackwell, 2002), 123–4.

2 Placing Africville: The Making of the Slum

1 Edward Said, *Culture and Imperialism* (New York: Vintage, 1994), 7.
2 Henri Lefebvre, 'Reflections on the Politics of Space,' trans. M. Enders, *Antipode* 8 (1976): 31.
3 See Doreen Massey, *Space, Place and Gender* (Minneapolis: University of Minnesota Press, 1994).
4 Edward Soja, 'The Spatiality of Social Life: Towards a Transformative Rhetorisation,' in *Social Relations and Spatial Structures*, ed. D. Gregory and J. Urry (New York: St Martin's Press, 1985), 90, quoted in Robert W. Williams, 'Terrorism, Anti-terrorism, and the Normative Boundaries of the U.S. Polity: The Spatiality of Politics after 11 September 2001,' *Space and Polity* 7, no. 3 (2003): 276.
5 Eugene J. McCann, 'Race, Protest and Public Space: Contextualizing Lefebvre in the U.S. City,' *Antipode* 31, 2 (1999): 163–84.
6 Edward W. Soja, *Thirdspace* (Malden, MA: Blackwell, 1996).
7 Charles Saunders, *Africville: A Spirit that Lives On* (Halifax: The Art Gallery, Mount Saint Vincent University, Africville Genealogical Society, Black Cultural Centre for Nova Scotia and National Film Board, Atlantic Centre, 1989), 17. Although the number of white Africville residents was small, they were reported to be well received in the community, and some white people moved in after marrying Africville people.
8 See, for example, Richard Thompson Ford's work on spatial segregation and how it is maintained 'from within,' even in the face of legislative policy that seeks to disband it. He describes how the infrastructure that is firmly instated by the dominant group makes it necessary for minority groups to maintain links to specific areas, networks, services, and other survival mechanisms, even when their socio-economic statuses change. Richard Thompson Ford, 'The Boundaries of Race: Political Geography in Legal Analysis,' *Harvard Law Review* 107 (1994): 1843–921.
9 bell hooks, 'Marginality as a site of resistance,' in *Out There: Marginalization and Contemporary Cultures*, ed. R. Ferguson et al. (New York: New Museum of Contemporary Art, 1990).
10 It is also the case that governments have always employed various policy measures, through zoning, construction, urban planning, and legislation around housing, to dictate and restrict settlement and to force community segregation. For a discussion of such policies and their effects, see for example, Kevin Fox Gotham, 'Urban Space, Restrictive Covenants and the Origins of Racial Residential Segregation in a US City, 1900–50,' *International Journal of Urban and Regional Research* 24, no. 3 (2000): 616–33; C. Silver,

'The Racial Origins of Zoning: Southern Cities from 1910–40,' *Planning Perspectives* 6, no. 2 (1991): 189–205; Thomas J. Sugrue, *The Origins of the Urban Crisis: Race and Inequality in Postwar Detroit* (Princeton: Princeton University Press, 2005).

11 See Steven Gregory, *Black Corona: Race and the Politics of Place in an Urban Community* (Princeton: Princeton University Press, 1998). For a more detailed discussion of the definitions and tensions of state imposed segregation and community agency, see Peter Marcuse, 'Enclaves Yes, Ghettos, No: Segregation and the State' (Lincoln Institute of Land Policy conference paper, 2001).

12 Michel Foucault, 'Right of Death and Power over Life,' in *The Foucault Reader*, ed. Paul Rabinow (New York: Pantheon, 1984), 262.

13 Ibid., 182 (emphasis added).

14 Michel Foucault, *Society Must Be Defended: Lectures at the Collège de France 1975–1976*, ed., Mauro Bertani and Alessandro Fontana (New York: Picador, 2003).

15 Eduardo Mendieta, 'Plantations, Ghettos, Prisons: U.S. Racial Geographies,' *Philosophy and Geography* 7, no. 1 (2004): 47, 49.

16 Kathleen Kirby, 'Re: Mapping Subjectivity: Cartographic Vision and the Limits of Politics,' in *Bodyspace: Destabilizing Geographies of Gender and Sexuality*, ed. Nancy Duncan (London: Routledge, 1996), 49.

17 Jane Jacobs, *Edge of Empire: Postcolonialism and the City* (London: Routledge, 1996), 19.

18 Audrey Kobayashi and Linda Peake, 'Unnatural Discourse: "Race" and Gender in Geography,' *Gender, Place and Culture* 1 no. 2 (1994): 225–43.

19 Kathleen Kirby, 'Re: Mapping Subjectivity: Cartographic Vision and the Limits of Politics,' in *Bodyspace: Destabilizing Geographies of Gender and Sexuality*, ed. Nancy Duncan (London: Routledge, 1996), 45.

20 Nicholas Blomley. 'Law, Property and the Geography of Violence: The Frontier, the Survey and the Grid,' *Annals of the Association of American Geographers* 93, no. 1 (2003): 128.

21 Mary Louise Pratt, *Imperial Eyes: Travel Writing and Transculturation* (London: Routledge, 1992), 7.

22 Patrick Joyce, *The Rule of Freedom: Liberalism and the Modern City* (London: Verso, 2003), 35.

23 Edward Said, *Culture and Imperialism* (New York: Knopf, 1993), 7.

24 Dara Culhane, *The Pleasure of the Crown: Anthropology, Law and First Nations* (Burnaby, BC: Talon Books, 1998), 48.

25 See also Ahmad Sa'di, who writes persuasively about how Zionists conceptualized Palestine as an empty land, conveyed in the notion of 'a land without people for a people without a land.' Ahmad Sa'di, 'Construction

and Reconstruction of Racialised Boundaries: Discourse, Institutions and Methods,' *Social Identities* 10, no. 2 (2004): 136.

26 Pratt, *Imperial Eyes*, 7.

27 Edward Soja and Barbara Hooper, 'The Spaces that Difference Makes: Some Notes on the Geographical Margins of the New Cultural Politics,' in *Place and the Politics of Identity*, ed., Michael Keith and Steve Pile (London: Routledge, 1993).

28 Gloria Anzaldúa, *Borderlands = La frontera*, 2nd ed. (San Francisco: Aunt Lute Books: 1999); Chandra Talpade Mohanty, *Feminism without Borders: Decolonizing Theory, Practicing Solidarity* (Durham: Duke University Press, 2003).

29 For a thoughtful overview of contemporary issues in feminist geography and the history of feminist thought in the discipline, see Lynn Staeheli and Patricia Martin, 'Spaces for Feminism in Geography,' *Annals of the American Academy* 571 (2000): 135–50.

30 Alison Blunt and Gillian Rose, *Writing Women and Space: Colonial and Postcolonial Geographies* (New York: Guilford Press, 1994), 5.

31 Ann Laura Stoler, *Carnal Knowledge and Imperial Power: Race and the Intimate in Colonial Rule* (Berkeley: University of California Press, 2002).

32 Ann Laura Stoler, *Race and the Education of Desire: Foucault's 'History of Sexuality' and the Colonial Order of Things* (Durham: Duke University Press, 1995), 113.

33 Mary Louise Fellows and Sherene H. Razack, 'The Race to Innocence: Confronting Hierarchical Relations among Women,' *Journal of Gender, Race and Justice* 1, no. 2 (1998): 348.

34 Sherene Razack, 'Race, Space and Prostitution: The Making of the Bourgeois Subject,' *Canadian Journal of Women and the Law* 10 (1998): 338–76.

35 Evelyn Brooks Higginbotham, 'African-American Women's History and the Metalanguage of Race,' *Signs* 17, no. 2 (1992): 261.

36 A common form of employment for Africville women was as maids in white Halifax homes. See Susan Precious, 'The Women of Africville: Race and Gender in Postwar Halifax (Nova Scotia)' (master's thesis, Queen's University, 1998); see also Evelyn Nakano Glenn, 'From Servitude to Service Work: Historical Continuities in the Racial Division of Paid Reproductive Labour,' *Signs* 18, no. 1 (1992): 1–43; Higginbotham, 'Metalanguage of Race'; Rhonda M. Williams and Carla L. Peterson, 'The Color of Memory: Interpreting Twentieth-Century U.S. Social Policy from a Nineteenth-Century Perspective,' *Feminist Studies* 24, no. 1 (1998): 7–25.

37 Higginbotham, 'Metalanguage of Race,' 257–8; Janet Guilford and Suzanne Morton, ed., *Separate Spheres: Women's Worlds in the 19th Century Maritimes*

(Fredericton: Acadiensis Press, 1994). For black women's views of white women in historical domestic relations and in feminist movement, see bell hooks, 'Sisterhood: Political Solidarity Between Women,' in *Feminist Theory from Margin to Center* (Boston: South End Press, 1984).

38 Peter Jackson, 'Policing Difference: "Race" and Crime in Metropolitan Toronto,' in *Constructions of Race, Place and Nation*, ed. Peter Jackson and Jan Penrose (Minneapolis: University of Minnesota Press, 1993); bell hooks, 'Representations: Feminism and Black Masculinity,' in *Yearning: Race, Gender, and Cultural Politics* (Toronto: Between the Lines, 1990); Paul Gilroy, 'Conclusion: Urban Social Movements, "Race" and Community,' in *'There Ain't No Black in the Union Jack': The Cultural Politics of Race and Nation* (London: Hutchinson, 1987), 223–50.

39 See David Theo Goldberg, *Racist Culture, Philosophy and the Politics of Meaning* (Oxford: Blackwell, 1993).

40 Mendieta, 'Plantations, Ghettos,' 46.

41 Rhadika Mohanram, *Black Body: Women, Colonialism, and Space* (Minneapolis: University of Minnesota Press, 1999).

42 Sara Ahmed, *Strange Encounters: Embodied Others in Post-coloniality* (London: Routledge, 2000), 54.

43 Puwar Nirmal, *Space Invaders: Race, Gender and Bodies Out of Place* (Oxford: Berg, 2004).

44 Evelyn Peters, 'Subversive Spaces: First Nations Women and the City,' *Environment and Planning D: Society and Space* 16 (1998): 665–85.

45 Kathi Wilson and Evelyn J. Peters, '"You Can Make a Place for It": Remapping Urban First Nations Spaces of Identity,' *Environment and Planning D: Society and Space* 23, no. 3 (2005): 395–413.

46 Edward W. Said, *Orientalism* (New York: Pantheon Books, 1978).

47 Goldberg, *Racist Culture*, 187.

48 Joyce, *Rule of Freedom*, 55.

49 Barnor Hesse, 'Black to Front and Black Again: Racialization through Contested Times and Spaces,' in *Place and the Politics of Identity*, ed. Michael Keith and Steve Pile (London: Routledge, 1993), 175.

50 Peter Marcuse, 'Not Chaos, but Walls: Postmodernism and the Partitioned City,' in *Postmodern Cities and Spaces*, ed. Sophie Watson and Katherine Gibson (Cambridge: Blackwell, 1995), 247.

51 Peter Stallybrass and Allon White, *The Politics and Poetics of Transgression* (Ithaca: Cornell University Press, 1986), 131.

52 Ibid., 132.

53 Goldberg, *Racist Culture*, 191–2.

54 Ibid., 190.

55 Kay Anderson, *Vancouver's Chinatown: Racial Discourse in Canada, 1875–1980* (Montreal: McGill-Queen's University Press, 1991).

56 Kay Anderson, 'Engendering Race Research: Unsettling the Self-other Dichotomy,' in *Bodyspace: Destabilizing Geographies of Gender and Sexuality,* ed. Nancy Duncan (London: Routledge, 1996), 208.

57 Stallybrass and White, *Transgression,* 125–6.

58 Ibid., 133.

59 Mariana Valverde, *The Age of Light, Soap, and Water: Moral Reform in English Canada, 1885–1925* (Toronto: McClelland & Stewart, 1991).

60 David Sibley, *Geographies of Exclusion: Society and Difference in the West* (London: Routledge, 1995), 24.

61 David Roediger, *Towards the Abolition of Whiteness: Essays on Race, Politics and Working Class History* (London: Verso, 1994). Also see Fellows and Razack, 'Race to Innocence.'

62 Razack, 'Race, Space and Prostitution.'

63 Stallybrass and White, *Transgression.* For further discussion of the persona of the *flaneur,* and particularly the gendering of urban space, see Anne McClintock, '"Massa" and Maids,' in *Imperial Leather: Race, Gender and Sexuality in the Colonial Contest* (New York: Routledge, 1995); see Janet Wolff, *Feminine Sentences* (Cambridge: Polity Press, 1990), for her analysis of the 'invisible *flaneuse*,' the female version of the male urban 'wanderer,' who often dressed in male clothing in order to claim the same privilege to access and explore the city. Wolff uses this persona to theorize how Victorian women were either excluded from urban space or could not occupy it without intense scrutiny of their status (for example, as prostitutes or 'loose women'), and of their class position.

64 Lindsay Bremner, 'Bounded Spaces: Demographic Anxieties in Post-Apartheid Johannesburg,' *Social Identities* 10, no. 4 (2004): 459.

65 Teresa Caldeira, *City of Walls: Crime, Segregation and Citizenship in São Paulo* (Berkeley: University of California Press, 2001), quoted in Bremnen, 'Bounded Spaces,' 460.

66 Mendieta, 'Plantations, Ghettos,' 51, 46.

67 Anderson, *Chinatown,* 187–91.

68 Anastasia M. Shkilnyk, *A Poison Stronger than Love: The Destruction of an Ojibwa Community* (New Haven: Yale University Press, 1985).

69 For examples of analyses in different sites, see John Bauman, *Public Housing, Race, and Renewal: Urban Planning in Philadelphia, 1920–1974* (Philadelphia: Temple University Press, 1987); Howard Gillette, *Between Justice and Beauty: Race, Planning, and the Failure of Urban Policy in Washington, DC* (Baltimore: Johns Hopkins University Press, 1995); Kevin Fox Gotham,

'A City without Slums: Urban Renewal, Public Housing, and Downtown Revitalization in Kansas City, Missouri,' *American Journal of Economics and Sociology* 60 (2001): 285. For critical sources on American urban redevelopment planning and issues, see Robert Fishman, *The American Planning Tradition: Culture and Policy* (Washington, DC: Woodrow Wilson Center Press, 2000); Michael Jones, 'The Slaughter of Cities: Urban Renewal as Ethnic Cleansing,' (South Bend, IN: St Augustine's Press, 2004); Liam Kennedy, *Race and Urban Space in Contemporary American Culture* (Edinburgh: Edinburgh University Press, 2000); Joe W. Trotter and Tera Hunter, eds., *African American Urban Experience: Perspectives from the Colonial Period to the Present* (New York: Palgrave Macmillan, 2004).

70 Arnold Hirsch, *Making the Second Ghetto: Race and Housing in Chicago 1940–1960* (Cambridge: Cambridge University Press, 1983).

71 Goldberg, *Racist Culture*, 198.

72 Allan Pred, 'Somebody Else, Somewhere Else: Racisms, Racialized Spaces, and the Popular Geographical Imagination in Sweden,' *Antipode* 29, no. 4 (1997): 398.

73 Statistics Canada, 'Population reporting an Aboriginal identity ... ,' http://www40.statcan.ca/l01/cst01/demo38a.htm?sdi=aboriginal%20population; Canadawiki, 'List of Nova Scotia Indian Reserves,' http://canadawiki.org/index.php/List_of_Nova_Scotia_Indian_Reserves.

74 For discussion of the problematics of whiteness as a marker of belonging in social space, see Linda Peake and B. Ray, 'Racializing the Canadian Landscape: Whiteness, Uneven Geographies and Social Justice,' *Canadian Geographer* 45, no. 1 (2001): 180–6.

3 Knowing Africville: Telling Stories of Blackness

1 Alderman, quoted in Donald H. Clairmont and Dennis W. Magill, *Africville Relocation Report* (Halifax Institute of Public Affairs, Dalhousie University, 1971), 272.

2 'Nova Scotia Hides a Racial Problem,' *New York Times*, 14 June 1964, 64.

3 David Lewis Stein, 'The Counterattack on Diehard Racism,' Maclean's, 20 October 1962, 26. Alan Borovoy conducted an informal phone survey and found that only two out of fourteen landlords were willing to rent to blacks.

4 'Interracial Marriages: Accept, but Don't Encourage – Churchmen,' *Halifax Mail Star*, 27 June 1966.

5 Donald H. Clairmont and Dennis W. Magill, *Nova Scotian Blacks: An Histori-cal and Structural Overview* (Halifax: Institute of Public Affairs, Dalhousie University, 1970).

6 'The Black Man in Nova Scotia: Teach-in Report,' sponsored by the student group X-Project (January 1969, document in archives, St Francis Xavier University), 9, 14.

7 Stein, 'The Counterattack.'

8 Donald Clairmont, 'Africville: An Historical Overview,' in *The Spirit of Africville*, ed. Africville Genealogical Society (Halifax: Formac, 1992).

9 David Theo Goldberg, *Racist Culture, Philosophy and the Politics of Meaning* (Oxford: Blackwell, 1993), 189–90.

10 Gordon Stephenson, *A Redevelopment Study of Halifax, Nova Scotia* (Halifax: Corporation of the City of Halifax, 1957), viii.

11 Ibid., x.

12 Arthur D. Angel, 'The Great Lakes–St. Lawrence Project,' *Land Economics* 34, no. 1 (1958): 222–31; Donald F. Wood, 'The St. Lawrence Seaway: Some Considerations of Its Impact,' *Land Economics* 34, no. 1 (1958): 61–73.

13 Stephenson, *Redevelopment Study*, 21–2.

14 Ibid., 27–8.

15 Donald H. Clairmont and Dennis W. Magill, *Africville: The Life and Death of a Canadian Black Community*, 3rd ed. (Toronto: Canadian Scholars' Press, 1999), 156.

16 See David Sibley, *Outsiders in Urban Societies* (Oxford: Blackwell, 1981), 30, for discussion of 'outsider' societies as antithetical to 'development.'

17 See also, H.S. Coblentz, *Halifax Region Housing Survey* (Halifax: Dalhousie Institute of Public Affairs, 1962).

18 Frank Doyle, 'Africville's Shackdom Shows Lack of Action,' *Halifax Mail Star*, 10 February 1965, 1.

19 Coblentz, *Housing Survey*, 22.

20 Specific reasons cited for displacement are land clearance, urban renewal, residential conversion to business use, highway development, and housing code reinforcement.

21 Coblentz, *Housing Survey*, 13.

22 Ibid., 25, 6, 26–8.

23 Furthermore, looking at photographs, I have been continually surprised at how unexceptional Africville housing appeared in the context of Nova Scotia housing generally. To this day there are white-inhabited villages in worse repair than many houses pictured in books and in the photo exhibit of Africville in Nova Scotia's Black Cultural Centre.

24 Frank Doyle, 'Africville's Shackdom,' 1.

25 'Africville District Takeover,' *Halifax Mail Star*, 1 August 1962.

26 Frank Doyle, 'Procrastination on Africville Should Be Ended,' *Halifax Mail Star*, 31 May 1963, 1; Frank Doyle, 'Attention to Africville Old Story,' *Halifax Mail Star*, 7 June 1963, 1; Frank Doyle, 'Suggests Action Soon on Africville,' *Halifax Mail Star*, 1 April 1964; 'Africville: Time for Action Is Now,' *Halifax Mail Star*, 23 December 1963.

27 Larry Bennett and Adolph Reed Jr., 'The New Face of Urban Renewal: The Near North Redevelopment Initiative and the Cabrini-Green Neighborhood,' in *Without Justice for All*, ed. Adolph Reed Jr. (Boulder: Westview Press, 1999).

28 Philomena Essed, *Understanding Everyday Racism: An Interdisciplinary Theory*, vol. 2 of Sage Series on Race and Ethnic Relations, ed. John H. Stanfield II (Newbury Park, CA: Sage, 1991), 13–14, with reference to Troy Duster, *Backdoor to Eugenics* (New York: Routledge, 1990), and Walter Rodney, *How Europe Underdeveloped Africa* (Washington, DC: Howard University Press, 1982).

29 David Theo Goldberg, *Racial Subjects: Writing on Race in America* (New York: Routledge, 1997), 15.

30 Bennett and Reed, 'Urban Renewal,' 187.

31 Oscar Lewis, *La Vida: A Puerto Rican Family in the Culture of Poverty – San Juan and New York* (New York: Random House, 1966).

32 Goldberg, *Racist Culture*, 200.

33 Daniel Patrick Moynihan, *The Moynihan Report: The Case for National Action*, ed. Lee Rainwater and William L. Yancey (Cambridge: MIT Press, 1967).

34 Bennett and Reed, 'Urban Renewal,' 189.

35 In Clairmont's study, residents cited lack of jobs and financial worries as by far the greatest challenges they faced. Familial problems were uncommon. See Clairmont and Magill, *Life and Death*, 207–46.

36 Susan Precious, 'The Women of Africville: Race and Gender in Postwar Halifax (Nova Scotia)' (master's thesis, Queen's University, 1998), see chapter 3, 'Work.'

37 Joyce A. Ladner, 'Racism and Tradition: Black Womanhood in Historical Perspective,' in *Liberating Women's History: Theoretical and Critical Essays*, ed. Berenice A. Carrol (Urbana: University of Illinois Press, 1987); Linda Gordon, *Pitied but Not Entitled* (Cambridge, MA: Harvard University Press, 1994).

38 Frances Henry, *Forgotten Canadians: The Blacks of Nova Scotia* (Don Mills, ON: Longman, 1973); Hyman Rodman, 'The Lower Class Values Stretch,' *Social Forces* 42 (1963) 205–15; See also Hyman Rodman, *Lower-Class*

Families: The Culture of Poverty in Negro Trinidad (New York: Oxford University Press, 1971).

39 Henry, *Forgotten Canadians*, 157–8. See also Donald H. Clairmont and Dennis W. Magill, *Nova Scotian Blacks: An Historical and Structural Overview* (Halifax: Institute of Public Affairs, Dalhousie University, 1970), which addresses this common stereotype of blacks and refutes it with regard to the Nova Scotian community they study.

40 Henry, *Forgotten Canadians*, 52, 162, 46.

41 Ibid., 111, 112.

42 For instance, a survey testing these attitudes asks whether 'coloured people should hate all white people.' Ibid., 133.

43 Stephenson, *Redevelopment* Study, 38–40. Note that he cites no studies or statistics on these presumptions; these parts of the report read like an informal, speculative conversation. Also see Bennett and Reed, 'Urban Renewal,' for a discussion of common theories about social pathology, including the alleged irresponsibility of parents in the ghetto.

44 Institute of Public Affairs, Dalhousie University, *The Condition of the Negroes of Halifax City, Nova Scotia* (Halifax: Institute of Public Affairs, Dalhousie University, 1962), 9–10, 19.

45 J.J. Kelso, 'Reforming Delinquent Children' in *Family, School and Society in Nineteenth-century Canada*, Susan Houston (Toronto: Oxford University Press, 1975), 290.

46 Stephenson, *Redevelopment Study*, 40, 38, 40.

47 See C.R. Brookbank, 'Afro-Canadian Communities in Halifax County, Nova Scotia: A Preliminary Sociological Survey' (masters thesis, University of Toronto, 1949), for speculation on the morality of black communities and the removal of children from homes.

48 See Stein, 'Diehard Racism,' 26, for discussion of the more covert racism emerging in the period, whereby white citizens perceive themselves to be non-racist and will not explicitly admit racist attitudes.

49 Stephenson, *Redevelopment Study*, 38.

50 Michael S. Boudreau, 'Crime and Society in a City of Order: Halifax, 1918–1935' (PhD diss., Queen's University, 1996), 415–82; for a detailed account of racism in the justice system, see Wilson A. Head and Don Clairmont, 'Discrimination against Blacks in Nova Scotia: The Criminal Justice System,' 4th report prepared for the Royal Commission on the Donald Marshall, Jr., Prosecution (Halifax: The Commission, 1989).

51 The lynching was prevented when the man was rescued just in time by police; he was never convicted of the rumoured offences. Boudreau,

'Crime and Society,' 425, 415–16. For discussion of the rise of Ku Klux
Klan activity in the Canadian west in the early twentieth century, see
Mariana Valverde, 'Racial Purity, Sexual Purity, and Immigration Policy,'
in *The Age of Light, Soap, and Water* (Toronto: McClelland & Stewart, 1991),
which also notes how white Canadian women in the Imperial Order
Daughters of the Empire (IODE) organization expressed fears over
white women's safety in a society with a 'Negro population.' Also see
William Calderwood, 'Pulpit, Press and Political Reactions to the Ku Klux
Klan in Saskatchewan,' in *The Twenties in Western Canada*, ed. Susan M.
Trofimenkoff (Ottawa: History Division, National Museum of Man,
National Museums of Canada, 1972).

52 Sheridan Hay, 'Black Protest Tradition in Nova Scotia: 1783–1964' (masters
thesis, Saint Mary's University, 1997), 147.

53 Boudreau, 'Crime and Society,' 434.

54 Ibid., 424.

55 Clairmont and Magill, *Life and Death*, 51.

56 Boudreau, 'Crime and Society,' 451.

57 Alan Jeffers, 'Black Activism Terrified RCMP,' *Halifax Daily News*, 11 April
1994.

58 Charles Saunders, 'RCMP Snooping No Surprise,' *Halifax Daily News*,
17 April 1994, 22. Also see Barry Dorey, 'Sorry Ain't Good Enough,' *Halifax
Chronicle Herald*, 21 July 1994, A1.

59 Reported in Alan Jeffers, 'RCMP Snooped on Rights Activists,' *Halifax
Chronicle Herald*, 11 April 1994, A1.

60 Ibid.; many names had been deleted in the files released to the press.

61 Barry Dorey, 'Sorry.' In this article, the couple wonders if the RCMP were
involved in the fires and ransacking; they state that the RCMP turned a
blind eye when the incidents occurred.

62 Edna Staebler, 'Would You Change the Lives of These People?' *Maclean's*,
12 May 1956, 30.

63 Many studies described their principal sites as 'the *most* depressed.' It was
frequently said of Africville, and also by Frances Henry of the villages she
visited.

64 It is never confirmed that residents actually have fears of being photographed for 'superstitious' reasons. For an excellent analysis of how blacks
in North America experience and reciprocate the white gaze, see bell hooks,
'Representations of Whiteness in the Black Imagination,' in *Black Looks: Race
and Representation* (Toronto: Between the Lines, 1992); see also Frantz
Fanon, *Black Skin, White Masks*, trans. Charles Lam Markamann (New York:
Grove Press, 1967); and Sherene H. Razack, *Looking White People in the Eye*

(Toronto: University of Toronto Press, 1998), which discusses the politics of the gaze in a variety of contexts, not only between blacks and whites.

65 For example, when a black child asks her not to take pictures, she spells it 'pitchers' in the quote, as if imagining he could not know the correct word.

66 During this period of time, *Maclean's* was aimed at a fairly affluent audience. Paul Rutherford, 'The Monthly Epic: A History of Canadian Magazines 1789–1989,' *Canadian Historical Review* 71, no. 4 (1990).

67 Frank Doyle, 'Dwellings at Dump Not Very Historic.' *Halifax Mail Star*, 18 January 1963, 1.

68 Frank Doyle, 'Suggests Action.'

69 Clairmont and Magill, *Life and Death*, 116.

70 Ibid., 122.

71 Ibid., 50.

72 Clairmont and Magill, *Relocation Report*, 123.

73 Ibid., 79, 194. See also Clairmont and Magill, *Life and Death*, 125.

74 Clairmont and Magill, *Life and Death*, 125.

75 Ibid., 120.

76 As Sherene Razack notes, 'What a spatial analysis reveals is that bodies in degenerate spaces lose their entitlement to personhood through a complex process in which the violence that is enacted is naturalized,' Razack, 'Gendered Racial Violence and Spatialized Justice: The Murder of Pamela George,' *Canadian Journal of Law and Society* 15, no. 2 (2000), 129.

77 Charles Saunders, *Africville: A Spirit that Lives On* (Halifax: Art Gallery, Mount Saint Vincent University, Africville Genealogical Society, Black Cultural Centre for Nova Scotia and National Film Board, Atlantic Centre, 1989), 17.

78 Henry, *Forgotten Canadians*, 156; 99–100.

79 Institute of Public Affairs, *Condition of the Negroes*; the authors never rule out the possibility that it may. In contrast to this doubt, 'The Black Man in Nova Scotia: Teach-in Report,' a few years later, cites various studies carried out during the 1960s and earlier that conclusively dismiss biological inferiority.

80 Institute of Public Affairs, *Condition of the Negroes*, 21.

81 Bernard MacDougall, 'Urban Relocation of Africville Residents' (master's thesis, Maritime School of Social Work, 1969), 18.

82 Susan Dexter, 'The Black Ghetto that Fears Integration,' *Maclean's*, 25 July 1965.

83 James Quig, 'Walking Black through Halifax,' *Weekend Magazine*, 19 June 1976.

84 Frank Doyle, 'Dwellings at Dump.'

85 Frank Doyle, 'Procrastination.'
86 Jim Robson, 'Africville Residents Want "Promises" Kept,' *Halifax Mail Star*, 3 October 1969, 1.
87 Susan Dexter, 'Black Ghetto.'
88 Mary Casey, 'Africville Awaits the Wreckers,' *Globe and Mail*, 25 August 1962.
89 'Nova Scotia Hides a Racial Problem,' *New York Times*, 14 June 1964, 64.
90 Hay, 'Black Protest Tradition.'
91 Judith Fingard, 'Race and Respectability in Victorian Halifax,' *Journal of Imperial and Commonwealth History* 20, no. 2 (1992): 169–95.
92 Coblentz, *Housing Survey*, 28.
93 Canadian Encyclopedia.com, 'The Influence of American Magazines,' http://www.thecanadianencyclopedia.com/index.cfm?PgNm=TCE& Params=A1SEC823875; Wikipedia, 'Maclean's,' http://en.wikipedia.org/ wiki/Maclean's. The population of Canada during the 1950s reached approximately 17,000,000. Statistics Canada, 'Population and Migration,' http://www.statcan.ca/english/freepub/11-516-XIE/sectiona/ sectiona.htm
94 Expert to Seek Solution for Africville Issue,' *Halifax Mail Star*, 13 September 1963, 1.
95 Clairmont and Magill, *Relocation Report*.

4 Razing Africville: Fusing Spatial Management and Racist Discourse

1 Then Halifax Mayor John E. Lloyd, quoted in David Lewis Stein, 'The Counterattack on Diehard Racism,' *Maclean's*, 20 October 1962, 92.
2 Public Archives of Nova Scotia, Africville File, document 1.
3 Ibid., 131.
4 Ibid., 134.
5 Donald H. Clairmont and Dennis W. Magill, *Africville: The Life and Death of a Canadian Black Community*, 3rd ed. (Toronto: Canadian Scholars' Press, 1999), 100. Clairmont and Magill, *Life and Death*, 100
6 Ibid., 109.
7 Ibid., 100.
8 Halifax City Council, *Minutes*, 9 September 1915, 211.
9 'Area Residents Anxious to Have Rights Honored,' *Halifax Mail Star*, 16 October 1962.
10 Donald H. Clairmont and Dennis W. Magill, *Africville Relocation Report* (Halifax: Institute of Public Affairs, Dalhousie University, 1971), 146.
11 Halifax City Council, *Minutes*, 17 September 1954.

12 Clairmont and Magill, *Life and Death*, 122–4.
13 Halifax City Council, *Minutes*, 16 May 1957, 338–9.
14 The prison was slated for removal and a new structure was to be built to hold all County, Halifax, and Dartmouth inmates. Clairmont and Magill, *Relocation Report*, 156.
15 Albert Rose, quoted in Clairmont and Magill, *Relocation Report*, 222.
16 Clairmont and Magill, *Relocation Report*, 163.
17 Ibid., 163.
18 Robert Grant, 'City of Halifax, Development Department Report, 23 July 1962,' in Clairmont and Magill, *Relocation Report*, Appendix A.
19 Gordon Stephenson, *A Redevelopment Study of Halifax, Nova Scotia* (Halifax: Corporation of the City of Halifax, 1957), 27–8.
20 Grant, 'Development Department Report', A4.
21 Ibid., A7.
22 Clairmont and Magill, *Relocation Report*, 163.
23 'Residents Want to Keep Homes,' *Halifax Mail Star*, 9 August 1962.
24 Clairmont and Magill, *Relocation Report*, 165.
25 Stein, 'Diehard Racism'; Clairmont and Magill, *Relocation Report*, 175; Howard McCurdy, 'Africville: Environmental Racism,' in *Faces of Environmental Racism: Confronting Issues of Global Justice*, ed. Laura Westra and Peter S. Wenz (Lanham, MD: Rowman & Littlefield, 1995).
26 Clairmont and Magill, *Relocation Report*, 377. The authors report that the majority of Africville residents said they had never had contact with the HHRAC; virtually none were involved in the planning process once the relocation program was underway.
27 Robert B. Grant to Donald F. Maclean, correspondence, 22 January 1963, in Clairmont and Magill, *Relocation Report*, Appendix D.
28 While this has not been stated openly by city officials, I noticed a shift in the discussion as relocation drew nearer. Later, in this chapter, I discuss the former mayor's denial that industrial development was ever seriously considered.
29 Clairmont and Magill, *Relocation Report*, 207.
30 Ibid., 210.
31 Ibid., 201.
32 Ibid., 203.
33 Ibid., 210.
34 'Expert to Seek Solution for Africville Issue,' *Halifax Mail Star*, 13 September 1963, 1.
35 Clairmont and Magill, *Relocation Report*, 214.
36 Ibid., 219.

37 Albert Rose, 'Report of a Visit to Halifax with Particular Respect to Africville,' in Clairmont and Magill, *Relocation Report*, Appendix F, A62. See also 'End Africville Blight,' *Halifax Mail Star*, 18 December 1963.
38 In Clairmont and Magill, *Relocation Report*, A62.
39 'Ontario Professor to Study Community,' *Halifax Mail Star*, 20 November 1963, 1.
40 The city paid Rose $500 for his ten-page report, which mainly echoed their existing views and plans. This was the same amount of monetary compensation offered to many Africville residents. Clairmont and Magill, *Relocation Report*, 227.
41 Ibid., 230.
42 Ibid., 231.
43 Charles R. Saunders, *Africville: A Spirit that Lives On* (Halifax: Art Gallery, Mount Saint Vincent University, Africville Genealogical Society, Black Cultural Centre for Nova Scotia and National Film Board, Atlantic Centre, 1989), 18.
44 Clairmont and Magill, *Relocation Report*, 246.
45 Ibid., 248–9.
46 Ibid., 267.
47 Ibid., 269.
48 Ibid., 376.
49 Mr. Carvery walked out of the meeting. After much negotiation, he insisted city officials come to his home to present him with a cheque. The city later issued a statement of regret over the coercive incident, but denied any ill intent. Ibid., 297.
50 Ibid., 274.
51 Ibid., 251–2.
52 Jim Robson, 'Last Africville Resident: If I Had Been a Little Younger City Would Never Have Gotten My Land,' *Halifax Mail Star*, 12 January 1970.
53 Clairmont and Magill, *Relocation Report*, 281.
54 Ibid., 150.
55 Ibid., 276.
56 These stories are also transcribed in Africville Genealogical Society, ed., *The Spirit of Africville* (Halifax: Formac, 1992).
57 Clairmont and Magill, *Relocation Report*, 194; Peter Edwards is a pseudonym used in the report.
58 Peter Meerburg, 'Africville More than Half Gone,' *Halifax Mail Star*, 24 June 1966, 3.
59 Clairmont and Magill, *Relocation Report*, 331.

60 It had long been a point of pride among Africville residents that almost no one in the community required welfare assistance. Ibid., 317.
61 'Says City Falling Down on Africville Project.' *Halifax Mail Star*, 26 April 1965, 1.
62 Clairmont and Magill, *Relocation Report*, 291.
63 Ibid., 310–12.
64 McDonough was leader of Nova Scotia's New Democratic Party (NDP) from 1981 to 1994, and of Canada's national New Democratic Party from 1995 to 2003.
65 Clairmont and Magill, *Relocation Report*, 326–7.
66 Jim Robson, 'Want "Promises" Kept.'
67 Clairmont and Magill, *Relocation Report*, 321.
68 Older community residents later stated that they had received rent for one month only. Africville Genealogical Society, *Spirit of Africville*, 88.
69 Jim Robson, 'Mayor to Probe Africville Claims; Seeks Way to Help,' *Halifax Mail Star*, 3 October 1969.
70 Jim Robson, 'Follow-Up Could Have Averted Relocation Problems,' *Halifax Mail Star*, 4 October 1969, 1.
71 'Woman Fined for KKK-Type Threat,' *Halifax Mail Star*, 22 February 1966.
72 Sheila Urquhart, 'Ghetto Going On Schedule,' *Halifax Mail Star*, 3 January 1966.
73 Ibid.
74 Clairmont and Magill, *Life and Death*, 226.
75 Ibid., 181.
76 Ibid., 215.
77 Ibid., 232.
78 Ibid., 226.
79 Ibid., 228–9.
80 Clairmont and Magill, *Relocation Report*, 337.
81 Ibid., 361.
82 Urquhart, 'Ghetto Going.'
83 This is not surprising as Africville was also known in some other black communities as a place to avoid; some blacks told Clairmont and Magill in interviews that their families warned them not to go there, and various people made distinctions between themselves and the Africville people, being quick to identify as residents of Halifax, not Africville. This suggests not only the powerful influence of racial discourses on racialized communities, but how differences in both socio-economic class and 'place' can be seen as one way, under extreme oppression, to establish a measure of 'respectability.' Clairmont and Magill, *Life and Death*, 255. For more on the

struggle for respectability as a raced, classed, and gendered phenomenon, see Mary Louise Fellows and Sherene II. Razack, 'The Race to Innocence: Confronting Hierarchical Relations among Women,' *Journal of Gender, Race and Justice* 1, no. 2 (1998).

84 David Theo Goldberg, *Racist Culture, Philosophy and the Politics of Meaning* (Oxford: Blackwell, 1993), 189.

85 Clairmont and Magill, *Relocation Report*, 377.

86 Ibid., 180–4.

87 Ibid., 181–2.

88 Ibid., 185.

89 See Hesse, 'Black to Front and Black Again.'

90 Goldberg, *Racist Culture*, 189.

91 Residents told Clairmont and Magill that the new apartment managers did not allow them to make small changes to suit personal taste without permission, and that the housing authority imposed strict regulations and sent inspectors into their homes frequently. Clairmont and Magill, *Life and Death*, 226.

92 Peter MacDonald, relocation social worker, quoted in Sheila Urquhart, 'Ugly Shacktown Going,' *Halifax Mail Star*, 8 March 1965.

93 Halifax Director of Development, quoted in Clairmont and Magill, *Relocation Report*, 234.

94 Bernard MacDougall, 'Urban Relocation of Africville Residents' (master's thesis, Maritime School of Social Work), 4.

95 Christopher Riou, '"Respectable Voices": Race, Class and the Politics of Progress in the Destruction of Africville' (master's thesis, Dalhousie University, 1998).

96 'Africville Settlement Must Go,' *Halifax Mail Star*, 11 August 1962.

97 Clairmont and Magill, *Relocation Report*, 373.

98 For more on respectability as a profoundly racialized construct, see Fellows and Razack, 'Race to Innocence.'

99 'Africville: Time for Action Is Now,' *Halifax Mail Star*; Frank Doyle, 'Suggests Action, Soon on Africville,' *Halifax Mail Star*, 1 April 1964.

100 'Africville District Takeover,' *Halifax Mail Star*, 1 August 1962.

101 Clairmont and Magill, *Relocation Report*, 234–7.

102 Dennis W. Magill, 'The Relocation of Africville: A Case Study of the Politics of Planned Social Change' (PhD diss., Washington University, 1974). Magill's dissertation resulted from this research, its text is almost identical to his and Clairmont's report. I have not used it separately from the report as I saw no place where it provided additional information or analysis.

103 Again, it is important to note that my perspective from three decades later is bound to be very different from that of researchers working in the midst of the fallout from such recent events. Hindsight always offers benefits, and the work of many critical theorists since that time has greatly influenced my analysis. Also, writing a critical book is quite a different project than is a report that has been commissioned by government officials for the purposes of documenting events.

104 Clairmont and Magill, *Relocation Report*, 303.

105 Urquhart, 'Ghetto Going.'

106 'Africville Move Slows,' *Halifax Mail Star*, 12 September 1966.

107 MacDougall, 'Relocation of Africville,' 73.

108 'In Search of a Sense of Community,' *Time*, 6 April 1970.

5 Reconciling Africville: The Politics of Dreaming and Forgetting

1 Andreas Huyssen, *Present Pasts: Urban Palimpsests and the Politics of Memory* (Stanford: Stanford University Press, 2003), 5.

2 Henri Lustiger-Thaler, 'Remembering Forgetfully,' in *Re-situating Identities: The Politics of Race, Ethnicity, and Culture*, ed. Vered Amid-Talai and Caroline Knowles (Peterborough, ON: Broadview Press, 1996), 190.

3 Lisa Yoneyama, 'Taming the Memoryscape: Hiroshima's Urban Renewal,' in *Remapping Memory: The Politics of Timespace*, ed. Jonathon Boyarin (Minneapolis: University of Minnesota Press, 1994), 103.

4 Jennifer Schirmer, 'The Claiming of Space and the Body Politic within National-Security States: The Plaza de Mayo Madres and the Greenham Common Women,' in Boyarin, *Remapping Memory*, 185.

5 Maxine Tynes, 'Africville' (excerpt), in *Woman Talking Woman* (Lawrencetown Beach, NS: Pottersfield Press, 1990), 62.

6 Charles Saunders, *Black and Bluenose: The Contemporary History of a Community* (East Lawrencetown, NS: Pottersfield Press, 1999), 205.

7 Joe Sealy, *Africville Suite*, Seajam Records, 1997.

8 Cited in CBC Radio One Maritime Magazine Archives April 18, 2004, 'Africville: Racism Reparations?' (accessed at: http://www.cbc.ca/maritimemagazine/archives/040418_africvilleReparations.html).

9 Africville Genealogical Society, *The Spirit of Africville* (Halifax: Formac, 1992).

10 Shelagh MacKenzie, *Remember Africville*, National Film Board of Canada, 1991, videocassette.

11 Jocelyn Dorrington, Nancy MacDonald, Pat Milligan, Joanne Syms, Nancy Sparks, and Lorne White, *The Spirit of Africville and Remember Africville: Teacher's Guide* (Halifax: Maritext Ltd., 1993).

12 For example, see Robert J. Britton, Letter to Halifax City Council, Re: Africville Genealogy Society, 28 October 1994 (Halifax Public Library, Africville file); see also Saunders, *Black and Bluenose*, 210.

13 Maureen Moynagh, 'Africville, an Imagined Community,' *Canadian Literature* 157 (1998): 15. George Elliott Clarke, too, has pointed to the Africadian cultural construction of Africville as a 'virtual community' for those who were unable to view it firsthand, in Saunders, *Black and Bluenose*, 9.

14 Moynagh, 'Africville,' 15.

15 See for example, George Elliott Clarke, *Fire on the Water* (Lawrencetown, NS: Pottersfield Press, 1991) a two-volume anthology of black Nova Scotian writing. Clarke's novel, *George and the Rue* (Toronto: HarperCollins, 2005) is a poignant history, based on true events, of two young black men growing up in poverty in rural Nova Scotia.

16 George Boyd, *Consecrated Ground: A Play* (Winnipeg: Blizzard, 1999).

17 It should perhaps be noted that this character is not based strongly on the real-life social worker. While the character is very young and inexperienced, directly out of university, Peter MacDonald was forty years old and had been practising social work for sixteen years. The character is from a wealthy Halifax family, whose strong social and political connections got him the job. MacDonald was the son of a steel-worker, thus working class, and grew up in Cape Breton. MacDonald does not appear to have discussed personal struggles or feelings of guilt when interviewed for the relocation report. This is not to say that MacDonald acted differently from or similarly to the character in his dealings with Africville residents, only that it is a fictional portrayal, perhaps designed to encapsulate a broader and more explicit black experience of white subjectivity at work.

18 The struggle for reparations to Africville residents is ongoing. Several supportive efforts have arisen since the initial research and writing of this work. A United Nations report on racism in 2004 called attention to Africville's history and requested reparations on behalf of residents from the Nova Scotia government. See CBC Radio One Maritime Magazine Archives, 18 April 2004, 'Africville: Racism Reparations?' Maureen MacDonald, a provincial New Democratic representative, has been actively urging the Nova Scotia government to issue a formal apology to Africville residents. In 2005, MacDonald introduced the Africville Act, a bill to this effect, entitled Bill no. 213, Injustices Committed Against People of Africville, in the Nova Scotia legislature. The text of this bill can be accessed at: www.gov.ns.ca/legislature/legc/bills/59th_1st/1st_read/b213.htm.

19 Deputy Mayor Pat Pottie, quoted in Charles Saunders, 'Africville Story Deserves Honorable Ending,' *Halifax Daily News*, 11 September 1994.

20 Africville Genealogical Society, *Spirit of Africville*, 98–100.

21 This is also confirmed in a quotation from the mayor's interview with Donald H. Clairmont and Dennis W. Magill, Africville *Relocation Report* (Halifax: Institute of Public Affairs, Dalhousie University, 1971), 240.

22 Africville Genealogical Society, *Spirit of Africville*, 99.

23 Ibid., 99–100.

24 Ibid., 101–102.

25 Ibid., 102.

26 The provincial government had promised, in 1991, to erect a replica of the church; the city, which now owned the space, was responsible for offering the parcel of land where the church would go. Saunders, *Black and Bluenose*, 220.

27 Britton, Letter to Halifax City Council, 5.

28 Ibid., 5.

29 Note that the people of Africville are often referred to as 'descendants,' although many of them were original residents. Most central activists in the genealogical society were middle aged at this time and had left Africville as teenagers or young adults. Various older residents were still living and were interviewed in the 1991 documentary. A major speaker at the 1989 conference was Ruth Johnson, whose great-grandfather was the first settler, John Brown. Ibid., 6.

30 These motions were not passed at this time, although the city had allegedly agreed to rebuild the church several years earlier. To the present day the church has not been built.

31 Saunders, *Black and Bluenose*, 207.

32 Ibid., 192.

33 Toni Morrison, *Playing in the Dark: Whiteness and the Literary Imagination* (New York: Vintage, 1993), 17.

34 Brian Underhill, 'Seaview Park Gets Go-ahead,' *Halifax Mail Star*, 21 January 1982, 1; Brian Underhill, 'Alderman Accusing City Staff of "Foot-dragging" on Northend Park,' *Halifax Mail Star*, 19 November 1981.

35 Lee MacLean, 'Seaview Officially Opens,' *Halifax Mail Star*, 24 June 1985.

36 Susan Lunn, 'Eyesore Transformed to Award-winning Park,' *Halifax Mail Star*, 7 June 1986.

37 Charles Saunders, 'The Dream of a New Africville,' *Halifax Daily News*, 3 December 1990; Charles Saunders, 'Battle Lines Are Drawn,' *Halifax Daily News*, 19 May 1991.

38 Charles Saunders, 'Africville: The Spirit Is Stronger Than Ever,' *Halifax Daily News*, 2 August 1992.

39 Cameron MacKeen, 'City Responds to Protest over Seaview Park Land,' *Halifax Chronicle Herald*, 12 May 1995.

40 Michael Lightstone, 'Africville Showdown Brewing,' *Halifax Daily News*, 12 February 1995.

41 Charles Saunders, 'The Law of the Land,' *Halifax Daily News*, 2 April 1995.

42 Shaune MacKinlay and Jim Rossiter, 'City Official Saw "Hurt," Carvery Says,' *Halifax Daily News*, 29 August 1994, 3.

43 Barry Dorey, 'Coopersmith Gets Tongue Lashing,' *Halifax Chronicle Herald*, 29 August 1994.

44 Cameron MacKeen, 'Get Out, Protesters Warned,' *Halifax Chronicle Herald*, 17 May 1995; see also Cameron MacKeen, 'Mayor to Act on Situation at Park,' *Halifax Chronicle Herald*, 3 May 1995.

45 Charles Saunders, 'The Law of the Land,' *The Halifax Daily News*, 2 April 1995.

46 Cited in Saunders, *Black and Bluenose*, 212.

47 Shaune MacKinlay, 'Africville Protesters Vow to Fight On,' *Halifax Daily News*, 31 March 1995.

48 Teena Paynter, 'City Gives Carverys the Boot,' *Halifax North End News*, 24 March 1995; See also Bruce Erskine, 'Africville Genealogical Society Backs Protesters,' *Halifax Chronicle Herald*, 18 May 1995.

49 Shaune MacKinlay, 'Scandalous,' *Halifax Daily News*, 23 March 1995.

50 MacKeen, 'City Responds.'

51 Michael Lightstone, 'Africville Lives as Rights Issue,' *Halifax Daily News*, 22 March 1995.

52 May Smith, 'Africville Protesters Haven't Left Park Yet,' *Halifax Chronicle Herald*, 1 November 1996; Brian Flinn, 'Africville Protesters Move Out,' *Halifax Daily News*, 31 October 1996.

53 Michael Lightstone, 'Ex-Africville Residents Squat in Protest,' *Halifax Daily News*, 14 August 1994.

54 'City to Clean Up Carverys' Seaview Park Camp,' *Halifax Daily News*, 24 May 1995.

55 Cameron MacKeen, 'Get Out.'

56 Michael Lightstone, 'Mayor: "No Racism in This",' *Halifax Daily News*, 25 March 1995.

57 Michael Lightstone, 'Africville Showdown.'

58 Cameron MacKeen, 'Halifax Alone Can Do Nothing about Africville Protesters,' *Halifax Chronicle Herald*, 31 August 1995, B3.

59 Kim Moar, 'Seaview Protester Arrested after Spat,' *Halifax Daily News*, 13 April 1996.

60 Charles Saunders, 'Scenes from Africville Reunion,' *Halifax Daily News*, 8 August 1999, 20.

61 Saunders, *Black and Bluenose*, 222.

62 Eugene J. McCann, 'Race, Protest and Public Space: Contextualizing Lefebvre in the U.S. City,' *Antipode* 31, 2 (1999): 163–84.

63 Samira Kawash, 'The Homeless Body,' *Public Culture* 10, no. 2 (1998): 319–39.

64 Henri Lefebvre, 'Monumental Space,' in *Rethinking Architecture: A Reader in Cultural Theory*, ed. Neil Leach (London and New York: Routledge, 1997), 142.

65 Huyssen, *Present Pasts*, 28.

66 It is worth considering whether city officials and others involved in the Africville decision engage, to some degree, in what Renato Rosaldo has called 'imperialist nostalgia.' Rosaldo defines this phenomenon as a process of 'mourning for what one has destroyed'; other examples are the romanticization of Native traditions and art by white North Americans, or the North American men's movement's reverence for a return to nature and the appropriation of Aboriginal rituals which they believe embody Other cultures, but without consciousness of their positions within the power relations which objectify, commodify, and destroy these cultures. Such positions seem possible when reviewing the comments of officials, in the documentary film *Remember Africville*, about their renewed valuation of community and their certainty that Africville would be treated more deferentially today. See Renato Rosaldo, 'Imperialist Nostalgia,' *Representations* 26 (1989): 107–22. See also, Jennifer Nelson, 'In or Out of the Men's Movement: Subjectivity, Otherness and Anti-Sexist Work,' *Canadian Journal of Education* 25, no. 2 (2000): 126–38.

67 Jane Jacobs, 'Resisting Reconciliation: The Secret Geographies of (Post)colonial Australia,' in *Geographies of Resistance*, ed. Steve Pile and Michael Keith (London: Routledge, 1997), 206.

68 Huyssen, *Present Pasts*, 101.

69 Ibid., 101–2

70 Jacobs, 'Resisting Reconciliation,' 214.

Afterword

1 Rick Conrad, 'Black Loyalist Heritage Society's Office in Birchtown Burned,' *Halifax Chronicle Herald*, 8 April 2006. The Dartmouth centre has since been repaired, and extensive efforts are being made to restore Birchtown's twenty-year archive of documents, records, and photographs on black history. There are also plans to rebuild the Birchtown office. Later in 2006, a man was charged with arson in the Birchtown fire. I have been unable to find any source commenting on his motivations.

See Mark Roberts, 'Shelburne RCMP charge alleged Black Loyalist arsonist,' *Coast Guard* (Shelburne, NS), 5 December 2006, 1.
2 John O. Calmore, 'Race/Ism Lost and Found: The Fair Housing Act at Thirty,' *University of Miami Law Review* 52, 4 (1998): 1069.

Index

of the Other, 41, 46; present day, 26; production, 22–3, 77; relation to power, 14, 55; ways of knowing, 36
Kobayashi, Audrey, 35
Ku Klux Klan, 66, 163–4n51

labour and class struggles, 15
lady, 38, 63; meaning in social space, 39
land: Africville, 7, 33, 59, 125–6, 132, 142; appropriation from Native peoples, 8, 11, 35, 142; federal legislation on use, 58; ownership, 11, 13, 92–3, 121, 152n13; white people's self-proclaimed right to, 28. *See also* space
Lefebvre, Henri, 29–31, 35, 139–40
Lewis, Oscar, 61–2
liberalism: ideas about integration, 57, 99, 103, 109–10, 115; justifications for Africville's destruction, 23; positive goals that 'didn't work,' 106, 129
Life and Death (Clairmont and Magill), 125. *See also Africville Relocation Report*
Lloyd, John Edward (mayor), 87, 89, 126
Loyalist migration, 6, 8–9, 29; free blacks, 9–11, 52
Lustiger-Thaler, Henri, 117
lynching, 66, 163–4n51

MacDonald, Peter, 90–2, 95, 126–7, 172n17
MacDougal, Bernard, 105, 110–11
MacKinnon, Fred, 127–9
Maclean's, 56, 59, 69, 73–5, 77, 108, 125

Magill, Dennis, 109, 170n102; *Life and Death*, 125. *See also Africville Relocation Report*
Mail Star, 85, 109
mapping and naming, 35–6, 46, 77
Marcuse, Peter, 42
marginal spaces, 20–2, 31, 46. *See also* borders
McCann, Eugene, 31, 139
McDonough, Alexa, 95, 169n64
media, 22, 66, 108; bias, 137; black voices, 124–5; calling for Africville's eradication, 60, 71; change in tone of, 124–5; coverage of Rose report, 89; descriptions of Africville, 12, 59–60, 71, 77, 80, 161n23; discrediting Africville's cause, 74; discrediting complaints of racism, 73; official story, 18; (producing) dominant discourse, 5, 16; racial discourses, 25, 55; racial narratives, 118, 140; racial stereotypes, 131; on Seaview Park occupation, 118, 134; small and alternative press, 75–8; supportive of city, 74–5, 106–7; white bourgeois family norms, 63; white fascination and revulsion, 70
memory and forgetting, 117, 130, 141–3; of Africville, 118; city's role forgotten, 100; white erasure, 149–50. *See also* commemoration
Mendieta, Eduardo, 33, 39, 48–9
middle class. *See* class
Mi'kmaq, 8, 11
Mohanram, Rhadika, 46; 'Black Body,' 39
Mohanty, Chandra Talpade, 37
monumental space, 141, 143–4, 146